September 11: Through the Eyes of a Child

By

Erica Craigston

ISBN: 1-4033-6176-2 (Electronic)
ISBN: 1-4033-6177-0 (Softcover)
ISBN: 1-4033-7772-3 (Dustjacket)

This book is printed on acid free paper.

1stBooks – rev. 10/25/02

Acknowledgements

Several people are responsible for this book. It took a great deal of effort from many people. If I have omitted anyone here, please accept my apologies, and know that your effort is greatly appreciated.

This book wouldn't have been possible without the contributions from the children and teenagers who put their hearts and souls into their work. I sincerely appreciate each one of you.

I owe a special thanks to Ms. Sharon Sumner, a teacher at Sullivan Elementary (Sullivan, Missouri). Sharon presented the project to the school on my behalf and successfully pitched my idea of getting Sullivan students involved in the book. Thanks, Sharon. You are the kind of teacher every child deserves, as you go the extra mile to ensure your students' success and self-confidence. Visit Sharon at http://eagles.k12.mo.us/sumner/.

Thanks to all the teachers at Sullivan Elementary for sending letters to your parents and encouraging your students to write. I especially want to thank Ms.

Sandra Painter for taking the time to make the book entries a class project. You made a world of difference.

There are several teachers, librarians, and webmasters that helped solicit writing and artwork for the book. I am grateful to each of you.

Thanks to Eric Vance for designing and maintaining my website. The site has been an important tool for recruiting young writers to participate in this project, and it will be equally important for promotions. Visit Eric at www.ericvance.net/webdesign.htm.

I extend my deepest gratitude to my friend and editor, Dr. Margie (MollyMarge) Snowden, who was instrumental in certain sections of the introduction and in her role as editor. MollyMarge, your editing experience blended well with your background in educational psychology to help me find the words to express several thoughts in various passages. Your advice and assistance are always appreciated.

I wish to thank the wonderful people responsible for the book cover: Razzy, Lynsae, Dawn, Bambi, and Faith.

Razzy Bailey (www.razzybailey.com), thank you for your photography work. In addition to your musical talents, you take beautiful pictures. Bambi, thank you for allowing me to share your granddaughter's innocence on the book cover. Faith, you were wonderful to sit still long enough to be photographed; it is difficult for a free spirit to sit quietly when there is such a big world to explore.

Dawn (www.creationsbydawn.net), you are truly gifted. Thank you for graciously granting permission to use the map/flag graphic displayed on the back cover.

Lynsae Harkins (www.lynsae.com), I couldn't have met a better graphic artist. I appreciate your taking on a project for which I had more questions than answers.

A special thanks goes out to Paul Crawl, my account manager at 1st Books Library. Paul, I appreciate your answering my never-ending questions.

Thanks, Eric C., for planting the idea for this book in my head, but most of all, thank you for your love and support. Together, you and Bambi polished the title, for which I am grateful.

Thanks to Catherine, my mother, for taking care of my animals while I dedicated my time to this book. Thanks, too, to my cousin Robert for tending to the yard and the dozens of other tasks. I hope to repay you someday.

Brandon, I am proud to call you my son. Thanks for being you.

Book Proceeds

Proceeds from the sale of this book will benefit several charities. Because children are at the core of this project, I have chosen recipient organizations that offer September 11th funds specifically for children and several educational projects that benefit youngsters.

Twin Towers Orphan Fund, Tennessee Farm Bureau's Ag in the Classroom, Tennessee's Overton County Library, and Missouri's Sullivan Public Schools are among the non-profits receiving proceeds.

While there is no confirmed number of children orphaned by the 9/11 attacks, Twin Towers Orphan Fund has 825 children registered with their organization. It is the organization's intention to actively pursue funding over the next twenty years to ensure each orphan's college education and to provide long-term health care support. Please visit this commendable organization at www.ttof.org.

I am happy to include a public school district and library among the fund recipients. These institutions often find themselves among the first to suffer reduced appropriations or be denied resource increases whenever public funding is scrutinized or budget cuts are imminent. Visit Sullivan Public Schools at http://eagles.k12.mo.us/ and Overton County Library at www.overtoncolibrary.com.

I have enjoyed several years of friendship with the folks at the Tennessee Farm Bureau. My friend Charles Curtis, Director of Special Programs, oversees the Agriculture in the Classroom project. This admirable project provides teacher training, materials, and workshops that assist teachers in communicating the important lessons our children should learn about food, fiber, and our environment. For more information, please visit their website at www.tnfb.com/specialprograms/agclass.htm.

Introduction

The purpose of this book is tri-fold.

First of all, it is for children. It provides children a forum for expressing their thoughts and feelings about the events of 9/11. It is important for boys and girls to share how they feel and openly deal with emotional issues caused by stress and trauma. Some youngsters convey their most difficult and private issues through artwork rather than words; therefore, art is included.

This work is not only for those children who added to the content, but also for every child who contemplates the work shared by those who contributed their expressions and reflections. There are moments in life when one spoken or written word can tug at our heartstrings and enable us to hear a previously unplucked chord. This is my hope for all who take the time to share in the work presented here. Many of the stories within this book demonstrate a much deeper perception than I had as a child, and, sadly, more empathy and understanding than I sometimes display as an adult. Other grownups may respond similarly.

Secondly, it is for adults. It is my intention that we use this work to educate ourselves about how children think, feel, and respond. Since today's youth will be tomorrow's leaders, that's reason enough to be concerned with their current perceptions and views. Parents, use this book as a catalyst to begin a dialogue with your children. Let's find out how our children feel. Then, let's use this knowledge to intervene where necessary and learn where possible. Children are our future, and it's not prudent to ignore their views or turn a deaf ear to their voices. When generations communicate what's on their hearts and minds, people gain mutual benefits from each other.

Thirdly, it's for charity. It offers readers, as well as all the children who contributed their heartfelt work, an opportunity to provide financial support to deserving agencies. Partial proceeds from the sale of this book will be designated as charitable donations.

It takes a village to raise a child. This adage applies here. To paraphrase, it sometimes takes a nation to write a book. This is not only my book. It belongs to citizens of the world— those who directly contributed work and those who unknowingly provided reference material through their journalistic efforts as well as those who read the book and allow it to touch their hearts. I've been blessed to have the privilege of pulling it all together.

Timeline of Events
September 11, 2001

Tuesday morning

7:59 Eleven members of the American Airlines Flight 11 crew depart Logan International Airport in Boston. Eighty-one passengers are aboard.

8:01 In Newark, New Jersey, forty-five people leave on United Airlines Flight 93, headed for San Francisco.

8:10 American Airlines Flight 77 leaves Dulles International Airport, Washington, D.C., with sixty-four people bound for Los Angeles.

8:14 Fifty-six passengers are on United Airlines Flight 175, along with nine crewmembers, and they leave Boston planning to land in Los Angeles.

Hijackers, at least three on each flight, crush all intentions for the planes to land at their respective destinations. Outfitted with box cutters, knives, and no reluctance to kill in cold blood, they forcibly seize control of each aircraft.

8:45 It's unthinkable. American Airlines Flight 11 crashes in New York City. Dust clouds and smoke swell out of the top portion of the World Trade Center's north tower. Violently, the Boeing 767 pulls the tower apart. The puncture point approximates the 100th floor. The structure is on fire. The sight is beyond sufferance.

9:03 Before the damage to the north tower is realized, United Airlines Flight 175 crashes into the south tower of the World Trade Center. The Boeing 767 tears into the top portion, right at the 90th floor, and the south tower explodes.

President George W. Bush is informed of the crashes. The U.S.A. has been attacked.

Airports in New York City are shut down, by order of the Federal Aviation Administration. New York City's Port Authority forbids entrance to the city's bridges and tunnels.

9:30 President Bush declares: "apparent terrorist attack" on the United States. He orders a full-scale investigation of the plane crashes.

Evacuation of the New York Stock Exchange necessitates the suspension of trading.

9:40 For the first time ever, nationwide air traffic stops in the United States. The Federal Aviation Administration halts all commercial flights and requires all planes in flight to land. All non-military flights are canceled.

9:43 A Boeing 757 smashes into the headquarters for U.S. military intelligence in Washington, D.C. It's American Airlines Flight 77 that collapses the second floor of the Pentagon's west side.

9:45 Evacuation of the White House is deemed necessary.

The World Trade Center's south tower gives way. Without warning, the 110-story structure collapses. Massive clouds of smoke and dust mix with dense fumes, and heaviness hovers above the debris.

A section of the Pentagon collapses within five minutes of the total destruction of the World Trade Center's south tower.

A Boeing 747 crashes southeast of Pittsburgh, Pennsylvania. In Somerset County, United Airlines

Flight 93 crashes. Apparently, passengers aboard Flight 93 aborted the hijackers' intent to target the Capitol or Camp David, or possibly the White House. Facing imminent death, passengers called their family members via cell phones. Reports based on passengers' calls support authorities' presumption that the flight's intended destination of Washington, D.C. was blocked by Flight 93's travelers.

10:28 Dust covers downtown Manhattan as the World Trade Center's north tower collapses. The 110 stories give way from the top down. Remaining are piles of debris as well as clouds of powdered particles and ashes.

10:30 New York's Governor George Pataki declares a state of emergency.

11:02 Mayor Rudolph Giuliani of New York City orders the evacuation of part of his city, including the area south of Canal Street.

11:18 Both United and American Airlines confirm the crashes of their respective planes. And both airlines confirm our country's worst fear: no survivors.

12:04 Evacuation of Los Angeles International Airport.

12:15 Evacuation of San Francisco International Airport.

The borders of the United States of America are closed. Both the Canadian border and Mexican border.

Tuesday afternoon

1:04 At Barksdale Air Force Base, Shreveport, Louisiana, President Bush commands "high alert" status for all U.S. military installations worldwide. The president's goal: to "hunt down and punish those responsible" for the attacks on our country.

1:27 Mayor Anthony Williams declares a state of emergency in Washington, D.C.

1:48 Suddenly and speedily, President Bush is flown to Omaha, Nebraska, on Air Force One. Destination: Offutt Air Force Base.

4:10 The World Trade Center's Building #7 is on fire, due to damages sustained in the collapses.

4:30 President Bush returns to Washington, D.C.

5:20 The 47 stories of Building #7, World Trade Center, collapse.

United States' officials suspect that Osama bin Laden masterminded the terrorism, and they believe that Afghanistan is harboring him.

In Kabul, Afghanistan, explosions occur at about 2:30 a.m. local time. The Northern Alliance, which is fighting the Taliban regime, is presumed to be responsible for the explosions.

6:54 President Bush is in the White House.

8:30 President Bush addresses the nation, requesting prayers for the victims of the attack as well as for the victims' families. His promise: the United States does not differentiate between the terrorists who are directly responsible for the attacks and those who provide shelter for the terrorists who committed the acts.

Erica Craigston

September 12, 2001

Wednesday morning

10:30 Mayor Rudolph Giuliani's announcement: deaths from terrorism will be in the thousands.

10:50 President Bush's declaration: attacks on the U.S. constitute an "act of war."

Nine public servants are rescued from the World Trade Center's rubble—   six firefighters, three policemen.

8

Wednesday afternoon

Federal Bureau of Investigation questions several people in Florida and Massachusetts.

Evidence confirms that, indeed, the White House and Air Force One had been targets for the attack.

4:40 U.S. Attorney General John Ashcroft's announcement: hijackers of the U.S. planes were equipped with box cutters as well as knives. Many of the hijackers had received pilot training in the U.S.

The New York Stock Exchange remains closed. NASDAQ remains closed, too. The earliest date for the exchanges' reopening is Friday, September 14.

Before Jeremy Click died in the Pennsylvania plane crash, he contacted family members via a mobile phone and told them about the passengers overtaking the hijackers.

11:04 At Kennedy Airport, police arrest a man carrying fake identity papers. Law enforcement authorities detain nine others.

The F.B.I. gives out search warrants as they hunt perpetrators in Florida.

9

September 13, 2001

Thursday morning

President and First Lady Bush visit Pentagon workers being treated at the Washington Hospital Center.

Rescue workers continue their search for World Trade Center survivors.

Confirmed dead: 94.

Missing: 4,763.

Crews continue to search for Pentagon survivors. As the fire is extinguished at the Pentagon, authorities estimate the number of victims, including the passengers of the airplane: 190.

The NASDAQ Stock Market, as well as the New York Stock Exchange, is closed.

Thursday afternoon

Authorities recover the flight data recorder from the plane crash at the Pentagon. The recorder appears to be blank.

1:50 Fifty people or more appear to be directly involved in the attacks on the U.S.

In Pennsylvania, authorities locate the flight data recorder from United Flight 93.

6:40 President Bush remains at the White House. As a measure of caution, Vice President Dick Cheney travels to Camp David.

Suspected bombers are detained by Philippine authorities, as the possibility of their connection to the acts of terrorism is investigated.

September 14, 2001

Friday morning

Three major airports in New York reopen, as do airports across the nation. Logan International Airport, Boston, remains closed until stricter safety measures are implemented.

12:00 noon At the National Cathedral, President Bush gathers with four former presidents (Clinton, Bush, Carter, and Ford) for the National Day of Remembrance. Present and past leaders unite America in prayer.

Friday afternoon

Secretary of State Colin Powell's announcement: Osama bin Laden is the suspected "ring leader."

The F.B.I. identifies eighteen hijackers.

The National Football League cancels games planned for the upcoming weekend. College football games will not be played either.

Erica Craigston

September 15, 2001

Saturday morning

The U.S. Senate agrees to spend $40 billion for emergency conditions resulting from the attacks, and the senators authorize use of military forces to fight the terrorists.

President Bush agrees to call up more than 35,000 reservists. He goes to New York in order to evaluate the damage and extend moral support to New York residents.

In Kabul, Afghanistan, leaders of the Taliban expect to be attacked by the U.S., and they pledge to retaliate and seek revenge.

The United States reopens its airspace to foreign planes.

Afghanistan threatens to invade Pakistan and other neighboring countries that allow the United States to use their airspace or military forces.

Funerals begin to be held in New York for victims of the attacks.

September 16, 2001

Sunday

Memorial services are held nationwide in remembrance of those who lost their lives as a result of the attacks on the U.S.

Vice President Cheney's announcement: stock markets will reopen on Monday, September 17. Also, he encourages investors to purchase stocks.

Pakistan leaders send a delegation to meet with leaders of the Taliban. Representatives of Pakistan intend to discuss the matter of having Osama bin Laden handed over.

September 17, 2001

Monday morning

U.S. stock markets open their doors. The Dow drops more than 680 points, and the NASDAQ drops over 115 points. At the end of the day, the Dow closes below 9,000. NASDAQ closes below 1,575.

First Lady Laura Bush is present at a memorial service for friends and relatives of passengers on United Flight 93.

Flights are cut by U.S. Airways. Approximately 11,000 employees are laid off by U.S. Airways. These layoffs come less than two days after Continental Airlines reduced their staff by 12,000 employees (on Saturday, September 15).

Taliban leaders debate stipulations under which they will deport Osama bin Laden. The United States, of course, is not one of the countries under discussion to receive him.

Monday evening

Attorney General John Ashcroft's announcement: the F.B.I. is investigating 47,000 leads and has 49 people singled out for questioning, while searching for an additional 200 individuals.

While visiting the Washington Islamic Center, President Bush censures acts of prejudice and violence aimed at Arab Americans and Muslims.

Major League baseball goes on.

September 18, 2001

Tuesday

Representatives of Pakistan leave. The Taliban asks for proof of Osama bin Laden's involvement in the attacks. Without evidence, the Taliban refuses to hand him over.

Airlines ask the U.S. government to bail them out of their financial deficits and take over the insurance liability garnered by claims.

September 19, 2001

Wednesday

The sudden descent of stocks continues. Officials talk about what's needed to reinforce the economy.

The United Nations cancels its New York meeting. At the same time, Boeing Airlines announces that 30,000 layoffs are imminent. Meanwhile, rescue crews in New York recover more bodies from the debris.

September 20, 2001

Thursday

In order to assist with the airline bailout as well as lawsuits filed against the airlines, President Bush asks the U.S. Congress for $5 billion.

Islamic clerics call for Osama bin Laden's departure from Afghanistan.

In the Persian Gulf, military forces of Great Britain join with the United States.

From the U.S. Capitol, President Bush addresses the nation and orders Afghanistan to turn over Osama bin Laden.

Epilogue

At the end of September, the number of dead or missing World Trade Center victims is reported as 6,412. The attack on the Pentagon resulted in the death of 184 people. As a result of the plane crash in Pennsylvania, 41 people died. By the end of September, 6,637 individuals were presumed dead, although this figure fluctuated in the months that followed. A confirmed fatality count has been difficult to establish.

The United States is forever changed.

The picture on the following page was printed in newspapers throughout the nation. The caption read:

Smoke billows from the Pentagon in Washington, Tuesday, Sept. 11, 2001,

after the building took a direct, devastating hit from an aircraft. The enduring

symbols of American power were evacuated, as an apparent terrorist attack

quickly spread fear and chaos in the nation's capital.

The photo, taken by Heesoon Yim, is reprinted by permission of Associated Press.

Why?

I'm not sure that anyone can fully answer the question of why 9/11 happened. There are academicians, historians, and politicians considerably more qualified to discuss our foreign policy and the Middle East than I, an average Jane. But then, isn't America made up of common people? I speak for many average people when I declare that what did *not* cause this atrocity are acts of commission or omission by the American people.

Of course, there is dissension on this issue. Anti-American sentiment may run deep in many foreign countries, but it hurts more when it comes from within. Some news accounts, books, and articles portray America as a rich, arrogant, selfish nation that blatantly wrongs other countries without regard for their citizens. I am not professing that we haven't ever made a mistake in our dealings with others, but show me a government that hasn't. America has provided a better life for more people than any other nation, both at home and abroad. Period!

Americans fund humanitarian efforts all over the world in an attempt to help less fortunate people. Generosity and selfishness are mutually exclusive. Read the paper; watch the news; check the Internet. You will find stories of the millions of dollars we have given and continue to give to help others. Despite the Anti-American words I hear and read, I have yet to see a mass exodus from our borders. That is probably because we enjoy relative security, freedom, and prosperity, and we will continue to do so despite September 11th.

"The best form of government that has ever been devised for protecting the rights of the people has been found to be the republican form. While not perfect, it nevertheless gives a voice to the people and allows them to correct the course of government when they find it moving in a wrong direction." <u>Thomas Jefferson</u>

"Be strong!

It matters not how deeply entrenched the wrong

How hard the battle goes, the day how long

Faint not— fight on! Tomorrow comes the song."

<u>Maltbie D. Babcock</u>

"In any project the important factor is your belief.
Without belief there can be no successful outcome."

<u>William James</u>

American Impact and Response

One book can't encompass every aspect of the impact of 9/11. But that's no reason to avoid an attempt to sketch the global view. I will touch upon some obvious, well-accepted changes in addition to some not-so-apparent issues below the surface. Together, let's explore our reactions. Then, let's decide which responses go overboard and which are lacking. Perhaps some are appropriately cautious.

More than anything, it is my hope that we will not forget our Black Tuesday. We must use our collective remembrance to honor the victims and strengthen our resolve to prevent an American future filled with fear, death, and destruction.

Erica Craigston

Immediate Responses

So many thoughts and feelings surface when we reflect on the moment we first learned of the attacks that fateful day— disbelief, anger, sadness, despair. Most of us were temporarily frozen by a debilitating fear that dictated our actions and consumed our thoughts. Life as we knew it had changed. Our skies were temporarily void of the usual ever-present planes. Trips were cancelled; events were postponed for days or weeks (including vacations, weddings, sporting events, and, for the first time in history, the Emmys). We were glued to the radio and television for news updates. For several days following the attacks, it was all we heard at restaurants, street corners, work, and school.

We were mortified about what our country was going through, and we gave freely to our fellowman during this time of need. Strangers comforted each other in the moments and days following the attacks. People who could scarcely afford it gave money to those affected by the tragedy; others stood in line for hours to donate blood. We came together strongly as a nation; for that, we should all be proud.

While we were consumed with thoughts of the attacks, we were also filled with patriotism. Almost immediately, President Bush declared the attacks an act of war against our country. Within a day, flags were flying from thousands of vehicles, businesses, and homes. Bumper stickers proclaimed, "United We Stand" or "Proud to be an American," and they donned every type of car from Mercedes to Volkswagen. American citizens waited alongside the rest of the world to see what our country would do in response to 9/11.

Nine days after the attacks, President George W. Bush delivered his Address to the Nation, in which he asked for Americans' continued support as our government, along with several other nations, began what was sure to be a long, difficult war against terrorism. Decisively, he attributed responsibility to the al Qaeda network, Osama bin Laden, and countries that harbor terrorists. He painted a grim picture of life in Afghanistan for those other than the terrorists, pointing out that Muslims and the people of Afghanistan are not our enemies; in fact, we are currently the single largest source of humanitarian aid to the region. President Bush stated in clear terms what would be expected— no, demanded— in terms of cooperation between the Taliban and the United States:

And tonight the United States of America makes the following demands on the Taliban: Deliver to the United States authorities all of the leaders of al Qaeda who hide in your land. Release all foreign nationals, including American citizens, you have unjustly imprisoned. Protect foreign journalists, diplomats, and aid workers in your country. Close immediately and permanently every terrorist training camp in Afghanistan, and hand over every terrorist, and every person and their support structure, to appropriate authorities. Give the United States full access to terrorist training camps, so we can make sure they are no longer operating.

These demands are not open to negotiation or discussion. The Taliban must act, and act immediately. They will hand over the terrorists, or they will share in their fate.

Erica Craigston

New Understandings

Our patriotic efforts were evident in the days and weeks following the attacks not only by our flags, bumper stickers, prayer vigils, and honoring events, but also by our increased commitment to give to our country. News stories reported that gallons of blood and millions of dollars were being donated in the name of 9/11. Armed services recruitment offices reported an increase in inquiries as some of our country's 55,000 reservists were called to active duty. Suddenly, Americans became interested in knowing armed services statistics, such as:

* At 1.1 million enlisted, our military force is smaller than ever, based on population.

* Even so, we possess the strongest military force in the world.

* 1.1 million service men and women take care of the rest of us— 281 million people.

* Service men and women are far more educated than at any other time in history.

* During World War II, 12% of Americans served in the armed forces.

* During the Vietnam War, 5% of Americans served in the armed forces.

* Today, less than ½ of 1% (one half of one percent!) serve in the armed forces.

In addition to learning more about American defense systems and political make up, many of us began to fully realize that we are part of a much bigger world. It may have been difficult to have empathy for civilians caught in the crossfire in war-torn countries prior to 9/11, because that world seemed so far removed from our own. Not any more. We've felt our own losses and have, in a way, been forced to think about issues we'd rather ignore.

Erica Craigston

Some terms meant little to most Americans prior to 9/11. Now, we care about their meanings and listen more intently. A few of these are:

* Taliban— Radical Islamic faction that wishes to maintain control of Afghanistan's government
* Mujaheden— Afghan resistance fighters
* al Qaeda (Arabic for "the base")— Formed by Osama bin Laden, an organization of ex-mujahedeen and other supporters providing fighters and monetary support to the Afghan resistance
* Fatwa— Religious ruling
* Jihad— Muslim holy war
* Islam— Muslim world; religion characterized by submission to God and to Muhammad as God's principle and last prophet
* Koran or Quran— Islam's sacred text, considered by Muslims to contain God's revelations to Muhammad
* Muhammad— Prophet who founded Islam
* Mosque— Muslim house of worship

* Sleepers or Sleeper Cells— Foreign terrorists who portray themselves as normal residents, blending into the community until ordered into action

Our children will study these terms and more as 9/11 becomes part of our schools' history curricula. There are four major U.S. textbook publishers. Each of the four now offer books that incorporate the study of 9/11, including the famous photograph of firefighters raising the American flag above Ground Zero.

Erica Craigston

Children's Responses

Though Americans have generally felt safe in the United States (especially prior to September 11th), we actually live in the most violent country in the industrialized world. This violence spreads to our children, with homicide rates being the second and third leading causes of death among the age groups of 15-24 and 5-14, respectively. Still, prior to 9/11, most Americans thought they could protect their families by carefully choosing the situations in which they became involved and the persons with whom they associated. After the attacks, people no longer held this illusion of control. How can we ever feel safe again knowing that terrorists based thousands of miles away randomly killed thousands of innocent Americans? The answer to this question lies in our response to these events.

Fear can be debilitating— imprisoning a person in his or her home or interrupting normal daily activities. This is especially true of young children, because they often lack the skills to address the underlying factors. Youngsters don't differentiate between fact and fiction or between what involves them directly and what doesn't. When a tragedy occurs, adults should discuss known facts with children (being cognizant of each child's age and maturity level), helping to avoid speculation or exaggeration. Often, what a child imagines is more frightening to him than the actual risks.

The attacks on 9/11 may have had an especially profound effect on children of middle and upper socio-economic groups compared to those who reside in high-violence neighborhoods (typically lower income). Certainly, children of all groups were saddened and frightened by the attacks. Regretfully, those of the latter group are more conditioned to violence. This often results in a numbing effect, whereby people consider violence as typical occurrences. Studies indicate that more than 40% of at-risk teens reported carrying a weapon for protection, and more than 30% of them reported staying away from school or skipping classes because they are fearful of sustaining personal injury or death.

It is well understood that children learn what they see— including patterns of violence. Children need to know that these senseless deaths are not only tragedies because they happened on American soil, but because violence does not settle disputes or solve problems. Let's take the opportunity to teach our children alternate methods of addressing differences of opinions.

For children whose families have been directly affected by 9/11's tragedy, their needs reach down far below surface attempts to console and reassure. Tragedy has shattered the foundations of their young lives. It's impossible to exaggerate the necessity of ongoing comfort and continual assurance that life really does go on.

All of our country's children, even those not directly impacted, know that something has gone wrong, terribly wrong. They, too, were bystanders when terror blasted morning routines to pieces and obliterated normalcy. Their sense of safety has been shaken.

Adults must help boys, girls, and teenagers to regain their balance. Youngsters, regardless of age, need reassurance that their family members are okay (if it's true). They need to know that grownups will handle whatever happens within their surroundings.

Included below are basic guidelines for creating an environment conducive to recovery:

Stay calm. Speak in a quiet, peaceful tone of voice. Point out that community leaders and workers are doing everything possible to keep people safe.

Remember: young people take their cues from parents. They respond to adults' emotional reactions. To the extent possible, avoid the appearance of fear.

Carry on with daily structure as much as you can. To keep a comfort zone intact, maintain chores, bedtime routines, and daily courses of action.

Stay close. Parents' physical presence is their child's primary source of reassurance.

Be truthful. Stick to facts. Acknowledge that the situation is serious. Assure youngsters that it's normal to feel upset and scared.

Listen. Keep eye contact, and really listen. Encourage children to express their feelings and thoughts. Remember: there's no right or wrong way to express confusion and fear.

Take care of yourself. Children and teens look to adults to model appropriate behavior. Reinforce self-care actions.

Most of us will not likely forget our whereabouts the moment we heard of the attacks. This marked the beginning of a transitional period for our country and our families. Several factors may contribute to how our children handle these changes, including:

- Child's Age
- Ethnicity
- Parents' Reactions
- Teachers' or Other Caregivers' Responses
- Societal Ties

- Relationship to Victims
- Proximity to Attack Sites
- Prior Emotional Health and Experiences

Addressing each of these factors will enable us to communicate more effectively with our children during this transitional period. While it is easy to list each of these factors separately, it is far more difficult to categorize them relative to a child, because they are interrelated. For example, relationships to victims necessarily affect parents' reactions. Nonetheless, these factors are worth consideration.

<u>Age</u>

After a disaster, children experience emotional struggles. They are not immune from suffering. They may not initiate discussion, however, because they see adults' distress.

By the age of two years, toddlers experience worries more prevalent than before. For example, a toddler is more anxious than an infant when a parent leaves. They fear loud noises and darkness. Very young children lack cause-and-effect awareness, and their imagination becomes more vivid than before.

By age five years, children become more self-assured. Still, preschool children will be confused by 9/11 events. They'll be extremely susceptible to adults' actions and reactions.

Elementary school-age children need explanations, because they want to understand what happened and why and when and where and how. They may need to express their concerns through puppets, art, posters, etc.

Adolescents will feel vulnerable. They will care very much about the events, yet they might try to act strong. Since they tend to analyze the world in black / white fashion, they'll want to know facts such as who are the good guys / bad guys. They'll pursue discussions with each other.

Ethnicity

Some Arab and Muslim children found themselves the target of insults and harassment in the aftermath of the terrorists' attacks. Even Muslim children who weren't taunted after 9/11 may be afraid of becoming a victim in the future (of both harassment and further terrorists attacks). Additionally, these children may be worried about relatives still living in the Middle East, particularly if they have overheard adults discussing concerns about possible reprisals that Afghanistan's Taliban government could levy against relatives of expatriates who the government perceives as disloyal.

One facet of the Big Brothers Big Sisters of New York program to alleviate post 9/11 stress for children focused on showing kids that people from all ethnic backgrounds were killed by the attacks. This lessened the feeling of isolation and conveyed the message that the world shares our grief and concerns. We should take this opportunity to teach our children that judgments should be made on an individual basis and not against an entire race or nation.

Parents' Reactions

Some parents may be tempted to completely shield children from the possibility of future terrorists attacks or other devastating events. Even if this were the best solution (and I don't believe it is), it is almost impossible. Children do not exist solely within their parents' worlds, but live with outside influences such as television, school, and friends. If children have questions that aren't adequately answered at home, they'll seek out answers from others who may not provide explanations the parents want them to hear. Or they may make up outlandish answers in their own minds, especially younger children. Children are very sensitive to the emotional climate of their environment; not telling them anything could lead to their imagining something far worse than the truth, such as that their life is in extreme immediate danger.

In the face of adversity or trying times, children, especially younger ones, take their cues from adults. While the devastating acts of 9/11 have left most of us (regardless of age) feeling somewhat vulnerable, parents who take preparatory action can reassure themselves and their children that they are able to exert a measure of control— even when confronting tough issues such as terrorism.

What action can we take to prepare ourselves and exert a level of control over such unpredictable situations? We can educate our families and minimize our risk factors wherever possible. This education should include:

- Understanding the most likely forms a terrorist attack may take
- Being aware of the most vulnerable places for a possible attack
- Learning to be alert and aware of surroundings
- Understanding precautions to take while traveling
- Observing and reporting unusual activity, suspicious packages, or anything "out of the ordinary"

- Determining emergency evacuation procedures for public buildings, especially work and school (such as the location of fire exits, flashlights, first aid supplies and how to use them, the quickest way out of the building, being aware of heavy objects that may fall)

- Securing a family disaster plan which includes emergency contacts, emergency supply kit, a family meeting place and communication system, escape routines, plans for your pets

In addition to reassuring our children that we exert some level of control over our circumstances, we may also allay their fears by focusing on the positive projects in which people have participated to help heal our nation. People have reached out to one another emotionally, physically, financially, and through various venues such as memorials. This well-received support has been as important for the giver as to the recipient; it is an important part of the healing process and allows some closure.

Not all children are willing to share their feelings; such children present a special challenge to parents who must devise a plan for opening the lines of communication. As responsible adults, we have to find out what our children want to know and respond honestly and directly, keeping in mind the child's age, maturity, and emotional status. The true account of circumstances is probably a lot less traumatic than what a child dreams up.

Teachers' and Other Caregivers' Responses

Teachers and other adults who spend time with children may have as much impact as the parents do on how they respond to violence. While it is beyond the scope of this book to explore the critical work that has been done in the area of diagnosis and treatment of children exposed to violence, it is worth mentioning that such crisis intervention models do exist. For example, Robert Pynoos and his associates developed a post traumatic stress syndrome model that has been especially useful to professionals and children's' caregivers. Pynoos' model focused on identification of trauma symptoms by developmental level. I urge parents to determine how others charged with caring for their children handle events such as 9/11.

We need to come to terms with how others plan to interact with our children under tragic circumstances. Recently, some parents were upset at teachers who allowed their students to watch the 9/11 events unfold on television, while other parents questioned why students weren't allowed to see *more* coverage.

Teachers have a tough job and can't please everyone, but, as parents, we should take this opportunity to learn how potentially emotional situations will be handled, allowing us to respond accordingly.

Other Factors

Additional factors have shaped how our children responded to 9/11 and their potential responses to the changes that are ahead. A child's societal ties, relationship to victims, proximity to the attack sites, and prior emotional health and experiences are but a few of these contributors. Regardless of which factors and obstacles present themselves as we deal with the difficult tasks of regaining a sense of normalcy, we must remember to listen and let our children be children.

Erica Craigston

Our Children's Generosity

We should be proud of our children. They have reached out to help others during this crisis. America's children generously raised more than $4.5 million for America's Fund for Afghan Children. These funds provided much needed school supplies such as pens, pencils, crayons, paper, and recess toys for boys and girls in Afghanistan. Newspapers nationwide reported children giving up their time and money to make a contribution to a 9/11 cause. There were even some charities run completely by teenagers, such as Kids Helping Kids In Crisis.

This project is another example of children's generosity. Without their time and effort, this book would not exist. My life is richer for having met these youngsters through their words and pictures. I'm sure that you will share my point of view.

Their Work

One final note before presenting the work of the young people who contributed their time and energy to this book: This is the children's writing, and I am sharing it with you as it was presented to me. Expectedly, some of the younger children have made spelling, grammar, and punctuation errors. Don't be surprised to see "they're" for their, vault spelled as "valt," or negative spelled as "negetive." These errors pale in comparison to the messages contained within their words.

I have left each child's work exactly as I received it. Therefore, there are inconsistencies in presentation styles, including capitalization and indentation. I have corrected neither the children's handwritten work nor the typewritten copies, for to mince their words would defeat the purpose of telling the stories "through the eyes of a child." Any corrections that have been made were unintentional, with the exception of breaking very long passages into paragraphs for readability.

The Strong Patriotic Americans

By: Kelsey L. Richards (age 11)

I think this tragedy may and has made Americans more patriotic and or stronger as people and a United Nation. We can and will win a major war if there is one, which we hope will not happen.

I also think it will make us as Americans stronger and more patriotic because the Twin Towers where important emblems of our nation that should never be forgotten and always remembered.

I think that having made this plaque or memorial for everyone that had died shows our patriotism.

Now because of Osoma Bin Ladin our security systems are more compact and lock tight.

I think that everybody should get on with there lives but still rember the tradijic deaths of many medical workers, fire fighters, police, and many innocent lives.

3/20/02

The Strong Patriotic American's

By Kelsey Richards

I think this tragedy may and has made Americans more patriotic and or stronger as people and a United Nation. We can and will win a major war if there is one, which we hope will not happen.

I also think it will make us as Americans stronger and more patriotic because the Twin Towers where important emblems of our nation that should never be forgotten and always remembered.

I think that having made this plaque or memorial for everyone that had died shows our patriotism.

Now because of Osoma Bin Laldin our security systems are more compact and lock tight.

I think that everybody should get on with there lives but still remben the tradjic deaths of many medical workers, fire fighters, police, and many innocent lives.

By Kelsey Richards

Erica Craigston

September 11

By: Alex Witt (age 11)

September 10
And all through the nation,
We had what we needed;
No need to ration.

Then the next day
The enemy struck,
Leaving the U.S
In one giant rut.

The stock market crashed,
The gas prices flew,
What happened next,
Nobody knew.

The President was "safe",
And the people were scared,
The toll was so many,
The citizens in despair.

56

The nation came together
Like a huge land,
And patriotism grew
Throughout the land.

We took out our flags and poles
Though covered with rust,
And stood true to our motto:
"In God do we trust."

"Nothing can bring you peace but yourself." Ralph Waldo Emerson

"Injustice anywhere is a threat to justice everywhere." William James

September 11

September 10 and all through
the nation,
We had what we needed; no
need to ration.

Then the next day the enemy
struck,
Leaving the U.S. in one giant
rut.

The stock market crashed, the
gas prices flew,
What would happen next nobody
knew.

The president was "safe", and the
people were scared,
The toll was so many the
citizens in despair.

The nation came together like
a huge band,
And patriotism grew throughout
the land.

We took out our flags and
poles though covered with rust,
And stood true to our
motto: "In God do we trust."

                              -Alex Witt

The following letter is by Jaclyn Bailey, age ten. She reflected on how she would feel if she had lost her parents in the World Trade Center attack. From her writing, it is clear that our children have thought about the details of 9/11 and considered how it may have impacted other children.

Dear America,

My triplet sisters and I lost are father and mother in the September tradgety. We will tell you America, it was tough when we watched T.V. in Mr. Wyatts room, seeing the World Trade Center colapse. My sisters and I fell to tears, thinking that our mother and father were in there and could not get out. We now live with our aunt and uncle. We have a story to tell, that nobody has ever told. Heres how it goes.

When we saw this we rushed out of school. We saw people just screaming and saying "OH MY GOD!" In the World Trade Center you could hear peoples bodies slaming into the ground, they had jumped. They thought we are going to die, some didn't some did. Firefighters had come all over the

59

United States. We have a uncle who lives in St. Louis he had to come down here in New York. We to now live in St. Louis, Missouri. But we will never ever forget our parents, or the day of September 11th.

Love, Jaclyn Taylor, and

Ashley Taylor and

Hailey Taylor

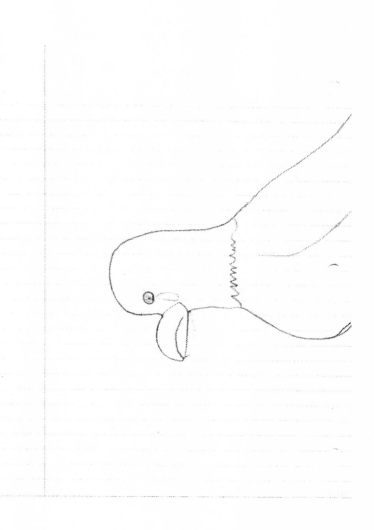

September 11

Anonymous (grade 5)

September 11, what can I say?
Many peoples lives were taken away

How could someone do such a horrible thing
Loads of their terror to our citizens they bring.

The Twin Tower and the Pentagon they have
destroyed
But with our minds, they have not toyed

They think their right but their wrong
Because all of American can stand
STRONG!

September 11

September 11, what can I say?
Many peoples' lives were taken away
How could someone do such a horrible thing
Loads of their terror to our citizens they bring
The Twin Tower and the Pentagon they have destroyed
But with our minds, they have not toyed
They think their right but their wrong
Because all of America can stand
STRONG!

Erica Craigston

64

"The Cart"

By: Devon Robinson (age 11)

Planes were coming
so close to the towers.
Only God knows what would happen
in the next few hours.

Then, boom, crash, bamb, shatter
was all we could hear.
People running, screaming
the end is very near!

They looked out their windows
not able to see
trying to figure out
what this could be.
America's darkest day
yet it was bright.
I guess that day
was wrong comeing right.

He thought he could scare us
and pull us apart
but he can't do that
because we have a cart.

A cart full of spirit.
A cart full of love.
This cart was surely
sent from Above.

"The Cart" " by Devon Robinson

Planes were coming
so close to the towers.
Only God knows what would happen
in the next few hours

Then, boom, crash, bomb, shatter
was all we could hear.
People running, screaming
the end is very near!

They looked out their windows
not able to see
trying to figure out
what this could be.

America's darkest day
yet it was bright.
I guess that day
was wrong comeing right.

He thought he could scare us
and pull us apart
but he can't do that
because we have a cart.

A cart full of spirit.
A cart full of hope.
This cart was surely
sent from Above

9/11 Essay

By: Nick Batey (age 12)

On September 11, he airplanes hit the world trade center. Another plane hit the pentagon in Washington D.C. Another plane hit into the ground and crashed in Pennsylvania.

If I had to speak to a child that lost their parent in the world trade center I would say that they are going to a good place with the Lord. To comfort them.

Before September 11, no one could buy a flag or anything. After the tragedy happened we could by thing that show patrism. An it happened to all Americans.

If I had to speak to a firefighter or a policeman or a medical worker that died in September 11, I would say that you did the best you could do in the tragedy. More lives were saved than were lost.

Some people don't like Americans and they think that we are selfish, too rich, and live in a fairy tale world.

Thank you to the firefighters, policeman, or any other volunteers for helping after the tragedy. You have courage because you saw things nobody should ever see.

On September 11, the airplanes hit the world trade center. Another plane hit the pentagon in Washington D.C. Another plane hit into the ground and crashed in Pennsylvania.

If I had to speak to a child that lost their parent in the world trade center I would say that they are going to a good place with the Lord. To comfort them.

Before September 11, no one could buy a flag or anything. After the tragedy happened we could by thing that show patrism. An it happened to all Americans.

If I had to speak to a firefighter or a policeman or a medical worker that died in September 11, I would say that you did the best you could do in the tragedy. More lives were saved than were lost.

Some people don't like Americans and they think that we are selfish, too rich, and live in a fairy tale world.

Thank you to the firefighters, policeman, or any other volunteers for helping after the tragedy. You have courage because you saw things nobody should ever see.

Nick Batey

September . 11 . 2001

By: Marvin Lumos IV (age 11)

On September 11 2001 I was really scared. I was deppressed too. Because every day at school my teacher talked about it and sometimes cried. I made me mad and hurt. I wanted to grow up now and be a good soilder and go over there and get revenge on them. I know God don't like war. Bible says so. So why does country different attack us? If they want to be like us then change thier country. Don't attack us or others.

"God listens to our weeping when the occasion itself is beyond our knowledge but still within his love and power." Daniel A. Poling

Erica Craigston

By. marvin Lunas II
3-11-02
age. 11

September. 11. 2001

On September 11 2001 I was
really scared. I was deppressed too.
Because every day at school my teacher
talked about it and sometimes cried.
I made me mad and hurt, I wanted
to grow up now and be a good
Soilder and go over there and
get revenge on them. I know God
don't like war. Bible says so. So
why does Country different attack
us? If they want to be like us
then change thier country. Don't
attack us or others.

Being Free

By: Christopher Williams (age 10)

Being free is making your own decision.

It's being able to vote, having rights.

Being able to be who you want to be.

It's being what ever religion you choose.

It's something that not every country has.

We should be thankful that all of those people died
in a war so we could have rights.

Being Free

Being free is
Making your own decision.
It's being able to vote,
having rights. Being able to
be who you want to be.
It's being what ever
religion you choose. It's
something that not every
country has we should
be thankful that all
of those people died in
a war so we could have
rights.

By: Christopher Williams

75

Letter to an Orphaned Child

By: Ian McCoig (age 9)

Dear Child

I've seen the news almost every day. I see osama ben laden laughing at all the people who died. Now it's pay back time. My prayers are with you and thouts.

Your friend

Ian

"We must dare to think unthinkable thoughts."

James W. Fulbright

"Never, never, never, never give up."

Winston Churchill

Dear, Child,

I've always wanted to be in the navy Because of what men things Osama Bin laden did. We will win because I know in my head. I wish you a happy and peaceful life

your friend
Traci

September 11th

Anonymous (grade 5)

Two tall towers
Up so high
Two tall towers
Proud in the Sky

Now you are gone
As we greive
We are a nation
This I believe

September 11th

Two tall towers
Up so high
Two tall towers
Proud in the sky
Now you are gone
As we greive
We are a nation
This I believe

Erica Craigston

9/11 Thoughts

By: Katie Strauser (4th grade)

If someone that is any color any color at all and they are getting ready to make fun of someone that is a different color than their color they should STOP and THINKand see how they would feel if someone else made fun of that persons color of their skin.

"We shall overcome, we shall overcome, we shall overcome someday. Oh, deep in my heart, I do believe, we shall overcome someday."

Civil Rights Song

If someone that is any color any color at all and they are getting ready to make fun of someone that is a different color than their color they should STOP and THINK and see how they would feel if someone else made fun of that persons color of their skin.

By: Katie Strauser

9/11 Essay

By: Nisie (5th grade)

If I were in the world trade center when the plane hit my building, I would have been frightened. I'd try to be one of the first people out of the building, running down the stairs as fast as possible without falling down.

While I was trying to get out of the building I would pray:

Dear God,

Help me to survive this tragedy and to see my family again.

On the way down the stairs my mind would remember how much fun I have with my family. How we like to laugh a lot and play tricks on each other. Sometimes we tickle each other until we can't take it anymore. We watch T.V., go to the movies, go to church, and listen to music together. At the end of the day, before we sleep at night, we pray and thank God for all the good things he does for us. When we visit my grandparents, aunts and uncles, and cousins, we have fun.

I enjoy going to midnight mass during the Christmas holiday. During easter we have an Easter egg hunt. If I were to survive I would thank God and write a book on the experience.

If I broke any bones during the collapse of the buildings, I could handle breaking any bones except my right hand because that is my writing hand. I love to write all the time. Whenever I have free time, I write short stories and e-mail my friends. Not writing until it healed would torture me to much!

I'm sorry for people who really did loose a family member. I bet they were thinking about you, just how I would have thought about my family. I know they're in a better place now.

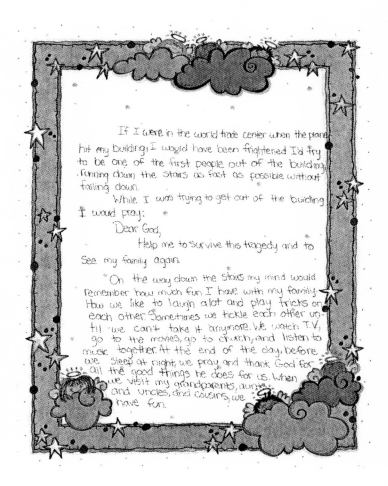

If I were in the world trade center when the plane hit my building, I would have been frightened I'd try to be one of the first people out of the building, running down the stairs as fast as possible without falling down.

While I was trying to get out of the building I would pray:

Dear God,

Help me to survive this tragedy and to see my family again.

On the way down the stairs my mind would remember how much fun I have with my family. How we like to laugh alot and play tricks on each other. Sometimes we tickle each other until we can't take it anymore. We watch T.V., go to the movies, go to church, and listen to music together. At the end of the day, before we sleep at night, we pray and thank God for all the good things he does for us. When we visit my grandparents, aunts, and uncles, and cousins, we have fun.

85

Erica Craigston

I enjoy going to midnight mass during the Christmas holiday. During easter we have an Easter egg hunt. If I were to survive I would thank God and write a book on the experience.

If I broke any bones during the collapse of the buildings, I could handle breaking any bones except my right hand because that is my writing hand. I love to write all the time. Whenever I have free time, I write short stories and e-mail my friends. Not writing until it healed would torture me to much!

I'm sorry for people who really did loose a family member. I bet they were thinking about you just now. I would have thought about my family. I know they're in a better place now.

~ Nine P

9-11-01

By: Amber Lindley (age 9)

When Sept. 11 came and I heard the shocking news, I just felt like it wasn't such a big deal. But when I heard the president decared war. Then It hit me that hundreds of children had lost thir moms and dads. And some children lost both.

I don't know what was going on in the hi-jakers minds. But I do know that they did not have Jesus in their heart. If they did have Jesus in their heart they would not have done what they did.

Erica Craigston

Amber
Lindley

9-11-01

When Sept. 11 came and I heard the
shocking news. I just felt like it wasn't
such a big deal. But when I heard the
president declared war. Then It hit me
that hundreds of children had lost their moms
and dads. And some children lost both.

I don't know what was going on in the hi-
jakers minds. But I do know that they
did not have Jesus in ther heart.
If they did have Jesus in their
heart they would not have done
what they did.

88

Dear September 11

By: Hailey Reid (age 10)

Dear September 11th why did you come why couldn't just skip it for fun?

Dear September 11th why did we get bombed?

Dear September 11th I have a question for you, why did dear September 11th spell out 9/11?

Dear September 11th that's all I want to know.

Dear September 11th why didn't you just skip it for fun?

Dear September 11

Dear September 11th why did you come why couldn't you just skip it for fun? Dear September11th why did we get bombed? Dear September 11th I have a question for you, why did dear September 11th spell out 9/11?

Dear September11th thats all I want to know.

Dear September11th Why didn't you just skip it for fun?

By: Hailey Reid

all?

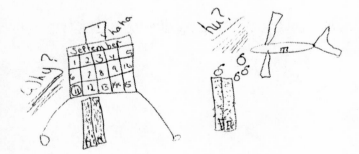

Letter to a Child

By: Stephanie Nye (5th grade)

If you could speak with a child who lost a parent in the World Trade Center, what would you want to say to comfort him or her?

Dear Child,

Hi, how are you doing? My name is Stephanie Nye. What is your name? I understand that you have lost one or two parents in the World Trade Center Attack. Are you okay? I would like to help you get through. Did you only lose one or two parents? Mom or Dad? Do you understand what happened to your parent(s)? How did your parent(s) die, in a plane or in the World Trade Center? They were both the terrorist falt. If your parent(s) died in the World Trade Center then they did not know, it was just a regular day until that happened.

I really do hope you get through. Your parent(s) loved you very much and they still do. Just think of them on a long trip and won't be back.

Who takes care of you now? Are you an only child? I am not. I have one brother (thank you) and he is a mean one. But, I would be very sad if I lost him. So, I really do hope you feel much better now, and understand that it was not their fault it was the terriost. Be mad at the terriost. Feel better!!

Your Friend,
Stephanie
Nye

"The life given us by nature is short, but the memory of a well-spent life is eternal."

Marcus Tullius Cicero

"Be bold— and mighty forces will come to your aid."

Basil King

If you could speak with a child who lost a parent in the World Trade Center, what would you want to say to comfort him or her?

Dear Child,

Hi, how are you doing? My name is Stephanie Nye. What is your name? I understand that you have lost one or two parents in the World Trade Center Attack. Are you okay? I would like to help you get through. Did you only lose one or two parents? Mom or Dad? Do you understand what happened to your parent(s)? How did your parent(s) die, in a plane or in the World Trad Center? They were both the terrorist falt. If your parent(s) died in the World Trade Center then they did not know, it was just a regular day until that happened.

I really do hope you get through. Your parent(s) loved you very much and they still do. Just think of them on a long trip and won't be back.

Who takes care of you now? Are you an only child? I am not. I have one brother (thank you) and he is a mean one. But, I would be very sad if I lost him. So, I really do hope you feel much better now, and understand that it was not their fault it was the terriost. Be mad at the terriost. Feel better!!

Your Friend,
Stephanie
Nye

Awaken the Giant

By: Beau Bartolotta (age 11)

On September 11, 2001 Afganistan hit us with two of our own planes by hyjacking them. They ran our planes into the heart of the twin towers.

When the first tower got hit people were yelling and running, people were crying, and some people just stood there, thinking about the future and the past.

When the second tower hit firefighters, policemen, and medical services were there who now people call heros. Most firefighters went up the two towers even thogh they all knew some of them would die and knowing this was going to be the most dangerous thing they will ever do. The rest stood outside pushing people out to safety. All those firefighters had a choice to do this but all of them offered to take the risk. Today people all over America work together to help restore New York.

Some people say Afganistan hit us to hard but for me I think they have just awoken an angry giant.

name: Beau Bartolotta   grade 5th   age 11
school: Sullivan Elementary School
teacher: mrs Paintner   number chosen 1

On September 11,2001 Aganistan hit
us with two of our own planes by hyjacking
them. They ran our planes into the heart of
the twin towers.

When the first tower got hit people were
yelling and running, people were crying, and
some people just stood there, thinking
about the future and the past.

When the second tower hit firefighters
policemen, and medical services were there
who now people call heros. Most firefighters
went up the two towers even though they
all knew some of them would die and
knowing this was going to be the most
dangerous thing they will ever do. The rest
stood out side pushing people out to safety.
All those firefighters had a choice to do
this but all of them offered to take
the risk. Today people all over America
work together to help restore New York.

Some people say Aganistan hit us
to hard but for me I think they
have just awoken an angry gant.

I'm Sorry For The Children

By: Jen Hess (age 10)

If I could talk to a little girl who lost her parents in the World Trade Center this is what I would say to her.

Listen, I'm very sorry. At least you know that your parents went to a better place. I'm sure your parents were very good people, and they did their part in life. I know most of all that your parents love you more than anything in the world, and they are just glad that you are safe. Believe me, I know how it feels to lose a loved one. I know that it's not easy. I lost my grandpa and he got everything for me. I know that your parents would want your safety more than their's. Don't worry your parents will always be living in your heart. That's something that you need to remember whenever you lose somebody you love. So now you know that they aren't gone. They will always be with you. I'm sure that you are furious at the people of Afghanistan, and you have no reason not to be. I'm posotive you will grow up to be just like your parents.

That's what I would say to her.

I'm Sorry For The Children

If I could talk to a little girl who lost her parents in the World Trade Center this is what I would say to her.

Listen, I'm very sorry. At least you know that your parents went to a better place. I'm sure your parents were very good people, and they did their part in life. I know most of all that your parents love you more than anything in the world, and they are just glad that you are safe. Believe me, I know how it feels to lose a loved one. I know that it's not easy. I lost my grandpa and he got everything for me. I know that your parents would want your safety more than their's. Don't worry your parents will always be living in your heart. That's something that you need to remember whenever you lose somebody you love. So now you know that they aren't gone. They will always be with you. I'm sure that you are furious at the people of Afghanistan, and you have no reason not to be. I'm positive you will grow up to be just like your parents. That's what I would say to her.

Dear Children

By: Erica Beckett (age 11)

Dear Children,

Hello my name is Erica Beckett. I understand that you have lost a parent. Would you like to tell me what your name is and your parents names. I feel sorry for you and I hope you can work around it. I'm going to ask you some questions okay.

Do you have a good life now that your parent/parents are not with you? Where do you stay? Did you lose both or one parent? When your sitting down is school do you ever mess up on your work because your thinking about them?

Now I have asked you some questions now let me help you here are some things you can do for your parent(s). Pray for them, work harder at school, and If you don't know exactly what happened to your parents ask a grownup, brother, sister, teacher, principal, or grandma. I have a friend named Sam Cook she has lost her father. Her dad had Lung Cancer. She has worked around it and I know if she can so can you. So I hope you have a very good life from your new friend Erica Beckett

Sincerly

Erica Beckett

Erica (2#)

Dear Children,

Hello my name is Erica Beckett, I understand that you have lost a parent. Would you like to tell me what your name is and your parents names. I feel sorry for you and I hope you can work around it. I'm going to ask you some questions okay. Do you have a good life now that your parent\parents are not with you? Where do you stay? Did you lose both or one parent? When your sitting down in school do you ever mess up on your work because your thinking about them? Now I asked you some questions now let me help you here are some things you can do for your parent(s). Pray for them, work harder at school, and IF you don't know exactly what happens to your parents ask a grown up, brother, sister, teacher, principal, or grandma. I have a friend named Sam Cook she has lost her father. Her dad had Lung Cancer. She has worked around it and I know if she can so can you. So I hope you have a very good life from your new friend Erica Beckett

Sincerly
Erica Beckett

Erica Craigston

How 9/11 Changed My Life
By: Amanda Higgs (age 9)

My daddy flys on airplanes a lot for his job. For a few days in September he could not fly or do his job then he could again.

When he is home I aske him where he is flying to and I aske him not to fly because he could get killed and we could miss him a lot. He says he has to. This makes me scared.

I was never scared before the attacks but now I am. I hope my dad doesn't get hi-jaked. We would cry.

"I come to the office each morning and stay for long hours doing what has to be done to the best of my ability. And when you've done the best you can, you can't do any better. So when I go to sleep I turn everything over to the Lord and forget it." Harry S. Truman

How 9/11 changed My Life
by Amanda Higgs

My daddy flys on airplanes alot for his job. For a few days in September he could not fly or do his job then he could again.

When he is home I aske him where he is flying to and I aske him not to fly because he could get killed and we could miss him alot. He says he has to. This makes me scared.

I was Never scared before theattacks but Now I am. I hope my dad doesn't get hi-jacked. We would cry.

Sept. 11, 2001

By: Rose Freeman (age 11)

Why do you think the Sept. 11th tragedy happened? I think September 11th happened because Bin Laden was jealous about us being a more powerful country than Afganistan and that we are free. I also think he did it because he wanted to be famous. I've heard he tried to blow up the World Trade Center before, but this time he blew up the World Trade Center, the Pentagon, and people believe that he tried to hit the White House, and he crashed a plane in Pennsylvania. But I think another reason is that the Twin Towers, the White House, and the Pentagon are important places in the United States, and if he blew them up everyone would know about it, and they did. I was really upset when I found out what happened, but I was even more upset when I watched 9/11. It was a sad movie. I hope it never happens again.

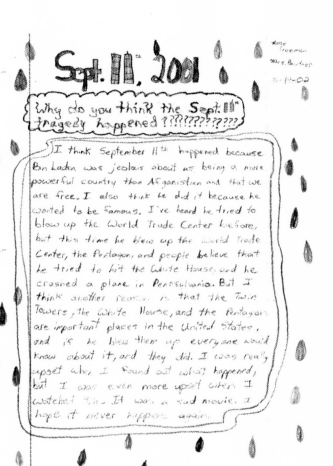

Sept. 11ᵗʰ, 2001

Why do you think the Sept. 11ᵗʰ tragedy happened ?????????????

I think September 11ᵗʰ happened because Bin Laden was jealous about us being a more powerful country than Afganistan and that we are free. I also think he did it because he wanted to be famous. I've heard he tried to blow up the World Trade Center before, but this time he blew up the World Trade Center, the Pentagon, and people believe that he tried to hit the White House and he crashed a plane in Pennsylvania. But I think another reason is that the Twin Towers, the White House, and the Pentagon are important places in the United States, and if he blew them up everyone would know about it, and they did. I was really upset when I found out what happened, but I was even more upset when I watched it on TV. It was a sad movie. I hope it never happens again.

105

Everyone Lost Something

By: Dustin Britton (age 12)

In my own words to describe what happened on Sept. 11th is that everyone lost something even if no one in your family died. Almost every body felt they lost something when the planes hit the World Trade Center and the pentagon, I know I did.

That day I felt like having the army go and blow up everything but I knew that wasn't the right thing to do because there are innocent people too. What happened was a massacre to our nation. What happened on Sept. 11th was something that should have never happened.

They hijacked four planes and only one missed. At the World Trade Center six floors was most likely three inches tall.

Dustin

In my own words to describe what happened on Sept. 11th is that every one lost something even if no one in your family died. Almost every body felt they lost something when the planes hit the World Trade Center and the pentagon, I know I did.

That day I felt like having the army go and blow up every thing but I knew that wasn't the right thing to do because there are innocent people too. What happened was a massacre to our nation. What happened on Sept. 11th was something that should have never happened.

They hijacked four planes and only one missed. At the World Trade Center six floors was mostlikely three inches tall.

Erica Craigston

Lost Mommy's and Daddy's...

By: Meagan Lindley (age 6)

I fill sad
because a lot of
babies lost their
Mommy's and Daddy's...

"When pain is to be borne, a little courage helps more than much knowledge, a little human sympathy more than much courage, and the least tincture of the love of God more than all."

C.S. Lewis

Erica Craigston

meagan fill sad 9-11-01
because a lot of babies lost mommy's and their Daddy's.

110

Wishes To Our Youngest Victims

By: Ian McCoig (age 9)

Dear Child,

I've always wanted to be in the navy. Because of what mean things Osama bin laden did. We will win because I know in my heart. I wish you a happy and peaceful life.

Your friend,

Ian

"Take calculated risks. That is quite different from being rush." George S. Patton

Dear, Childs

I've always wanted to be in the navy. Because of what mean things Osama Bin laden did. We will win because I know in my head. I wish your a happy and peaceful life

your friend
Love,

Essay on Patriotism

By: Alex Witt (age 11)

September 11, gory, scary, dazed. To say it all, the most horrific day any American has ever seen. But, after the initial shock we saw a new side of humanity. People joing together for an united cause, fighting terrorism.

Little children saved tooth fairy money to send to relief efforts in New York. School children wrote letters to fire fighters. Everyone was being more patriotic.

People need to realize the war on terrorism is not over, and to keep on being patriotic.

Erica Craigston

September 11, gory, scary, dazed.
To say it all, the most horrific
day any American has ever seen.
But, after the initial shock we
saw a new side of humanity.
People joing together for an
united cause, fighting terrorism.
    Little children saved tooth
fairy money to send to relief
efforts in New York. School
children wrote letters to fire
fighters. Everyone was being
more patriotic.
    People need to realize the
war on terrorism is not over,
and to keep on being patriotic.

                        -Alex Witt

The pictures on the following three pages were drawn by Sam DuBois, age six. The three sequenced drawings depict the following events:

1. A beautiful day in New York.
2. A jet heads toward buildings in New York.
3. A plane hits the one of the towers.

Erica Craigston

Erica Craigston

We Will Never Forget

By: Dillon Renfro (age 10)

On September 11 terrorists hijacked planes and crashed them into the Twin Towers. Then the towers fell and there was a silence in the U.S.A. After the silence was over we all worked together. We found some survivors and we found some that didn't.

I will make our country stranger and more patriotic because whatever happens once won't happen agin. And if we all stick together and stand together we can conquer this. If we all work together we can clean up the mess they left behind. If we can conquer this one of the many things that have and will happen in our country then we can conquer anything. If we fight back at the people that did this and the followers then we will of conquered this.

But we will never forget!

On September 11 terrorists hijacked planes and crashed them into the Twin Towers. Then the towers fell and there was a silence in the U.S.A. After the silence was over we all worked together. We found some survivors and we found some that did it.

I will make our country stronger and more patriotic because whatever happens once won't happen agin. And if we all stick together and stand together we can conquer this. If we all work together we can clean up the mess they left behind. If we can conquer this one of the many things that have and will happen in our country then we can conquer anything. If we fight back at the people that did this and the followers then we will of conquered this. But we will never forget!

By Dillon Renfro

One Morning

By: Darian Haffer (age 10)

I woke up one morning and I was putting my shoes on and my dad was watching the news and said two plans flew into the twin towers and the pentagon. I saw people on tv and Ben Laden. He was really ugly. I got really tired of seeing those ugly people on tv.

So I stopped watching tv. I started to watch tv again and we went to war and we have been fighting for about fifty-eight days and we haven't found Ben laden. But I think we are going to find him.

Darion
3d effl

I woke up one morning and I
was putting my shoes on and
my dad was watching the news and
said two plane flew into the twen towers
and the pentagon. I saw people on tv
and Ben Loden. He was really ugly.
I got really tired of seeing those ugly
people on tv.

So I stopped watching tv. I started
to watch tv again and we went to
war and we have been fighting for
about fifty – eight days and we haven't
found Ben loden. But I think we
are going to find him.

The   End

The Worst Day There Ever Was
By: Derek Harris (age 11)

What happened on September 11th was a tragedy to the whole United States. Many people died on that day and many people tried to save other people.

I think that that day was the worst day ever. I think if somone caught Bin Laden they should find a big field and put Bin Laden on a plane and crash the plane.

I think lots of people were sad on that day. I read a story about one of the parents of a child that was on the plane that crashed. The night before the boy left said, "Dad, I feel weird about riding in the plane."

The next day the little boy got on the plane and that plane crashed into one of the buildings. I think that that boy's dad was very sad. I would be sad if one of my family members were on one of the planes. I also want to thank all the cops, firefighters, and other people who helped with the tragedy. I feel very sorry for the family members that knew people who died. I just wish we could go back to that day and be ready for that Bin Laden guy and everyone could be out of the buildings and be safe. But I know that we can't do that. Like I said many people died and many people survived. That was the worst day there ever was. At least I think that.

Erica Craigston

<u>Derek</u>

What happened on September 11th was a trasedy to the whole United States. Many people died on that day and many people tried to save other people.

I think that that day was the worst day ever. I think if somone caught Bin Laden they should find a big field and put Bin Laden on a plane and crash the plane.

I think lots of people were sad on that day. I read a story about one of the parents of a child that was on the plane that crashed. The night before the boy left said, "Dad, I feel weird about riding in the plane."

The next day the little boy got on the plane and that plane crashed into one of the buildings. I think that that boy's dad was very sad. I would be sad if one of my family members were on one of the planes. I also want to thank all the cops, firefighters, and other people who helped with the tragedy. I feel very sorry for the family members that knew people who died. I just wish we could go back to that day and be ready for that Bin Laden guy and everyone could be out of the buildings and be safe. But I know that we can't do that. Like I said many people died and many people survived. That was the worst day there ever was. At least I think that.

9/11 Essay

By: Devon Robinson (age 11)

I was at lunch when I first heard what happened that day. The first thing that came to my mind was, "Oh my Gosh!". I automatically thought about my friend Jen Hess and her family. She came from New York in the 2nd grade. When I got back from lunch recess, our 5th grade teacher told us what happened. I didn't really understand what was happening. I didn't think it was that big. When I got home, my stepdad was there. I called my mom at work and she said she'd tell me what was going on when she got home.

When she got home, she told me what a terrorist attack was. Then, I called my friend Jan and asked if she had family near ground zero. She said no.

When I got in bed, I thought about my brother, Trent. I hoped he was okay. He didn't call our house that day. I prayed that he didn't get drafted.

The next day, I thought about my friend, Mike. I remembered that he just got out of the military. I was really worried about him, too.

Erica Craigston

Just about 3 months ago, Mike went back into the Army. Last I heard, he was doing all right. About a month after the attacks, I wrote this poem:

> "Early one morning,
> while we were working
> you hit our cities
> with our own planes
> I swear Bin Ladden
> if we don't find you
> in your world
> peace will never reign."

I was watching the president talk on T.V. I realized that Sept. 11 wasn't just a day of terror. I realized that on that gloomy day, America rose so high in spirit, not even the tallest buildings in the world could reach the top of this huge height of spirit America built that day. I can only think one word to describe that day, **PRIDE**.

Devon
Robinson

I was at lunch when I first heard what happened that day. The first thing that came to my mind was "Oh my Gosh!" I automatically thought about my friend Jen Hassan and her family. She came from New York in the 3rd grade. When I got back from lunch recess, our 5th grade teacher told us what happened. I didn't really understand what was happening. I didn't think it was that big. When I got home, my stepdad was there. I called my mom at work and she said she'd tell me what was going on when she got home.

When she got home, she told me what a terrorist attack was. Then I called my friend Jen and asked if she had family near ground zero. She said no.

When I got in bed, I thought about my brother, Brent. I hoped he was okay. He didn't call our house that day. I prayed that he didn't get drafted.

The next day, I thought about my friend Mike. I remembered that he just got out of the military. I was really worried about him, too.

Just about 3 months ago, Mike went back into the Army. Last I heard, he was doing all right. About a month after the attack, I wrote this poem:

129

Erica Craigston

"Early one morning,
while we were working
you hit our cities
with our own planes.
I swear Bin Laden
if we don't find you
in your world
peace will never reign."

I was watching the president talk on T.V.
I realized that Sept. 11 wasn't just a day of
terror. I realized that on that gloomy day, America
rose so high in spirit not even the tallest
buildings in the world could reach the top
of this huge height of spirit America built
that day. I can only think one word to describe
that day, PRIDE.

9/11 Essay

By: Cody Davis (age 11)

I think the Sept. 11 tragedy happened because some other countries are intimidated by America. Osoma Bin Ladin is a bad man. They should have caught and seized him when he struck the Twin Towers before. So he could not do it again.

Some people think it's because of airport security some say it's because Osoma Bin Ladin is just a bad man. I think it's because Osoma Bin Ladin is a bad man. Another thing is how did those highjackers get on the plane to highjack it.

Ok all those things happened and no sign of Bin Ladin. In my opinion we better catch him before he strikes again.

But don't worry President Bush says he is going to catch Osoma Bin Ladin.

Erica Craigston

Num: Cody Davis grade: 5th Age: 11
School: Sullivan Elementary
Teacher: Mrs. Bardner
Number chosen: 5

I think the Sept. 11 tragedy happened because some other countries are intimidated by America. Osama Bin Ladin is a bad man. They should have caught and seized him when he struck the Twin Towers before. So he could not do it again.

Some people think it's because of airport security some say it's because Osama Bin Ladin is just a bad man. I think it's because Osama Bin Ladin is a bad man. Another thing is how did those highjackers get on the plane to highjack it.

Ok all those things happened and no sign of Bin Ladin. In my opinion we better catch him before he strikes again.

But don't worry President Bush says he is going to catch Osama Bin Ladin.

Letter to a Child

By: Ian McCoig (age 9)

Dear Child

I am so sorry your parents died. I am praying for you. My thoughts are with you. I would be sad if I lost my parents. My wishes are with you.

Your friend

Ian

Dear, Child

I am so sorry your parents died. I am praying for you. My thoughts are with you. It would be sad if I lost my parents. My wishes are with you.

your friend
Stan

Erica Craigston

September 11

By: Stephanie Proffer (age 11)

When I first heard about what happened, I was at lunch. My friend came up to me and told me about the terrorists. At the time, I didn't think it was a big deal. When I got home, I started watching the news and they were talking about how Bin Laden hired terrorists to highjack four planes. But when I really got worried was when they said <u>WHERE</u> the planes crashed.

"The four planes appeared to crash into the Pentagon, the Twin Towers, and in Pennsylvania," said the news anchorman.

The thing was, my aunt, uncle, and two cousins live in New Jersey but they work in New York. Then, my mom called to see if they were all right, and unlike many of the people in New York, they were.

I think what happened on September 11 was devistating and I feel terrible for all of those innocent people who were killed and for families who lost loved ones. It doesn't matter what the reason was, whether it being that we don't practice the same religion that

Afghans, or because they envy us because they're a poorer country, there is no excuse for the tragic crime the terrorists committed on that September day.

Erica Craigston

SEPTEMBER 11

When I first heard about what happened, I was at lunch. My friend came up to me and told me about the terrorists. At the time, I didn't think it was a big deal. When I got home, I started watching the news and they were talking about how Bin Laden hired terrorists to highjack four planes. But when I really got worried was when they said WHERE the planes crashed.

"The four planes appeared to crash into the Pentagon, the Twin Towers, and in Pennsylvania," said the news anchorman.

The thing was, my aunt, uncle, and two cousins live in New Jersey but they work in New York. Then, my mom called to see if they were all right, and unlike many of the people in New York, they were.

I think what happened on September 11 was devistating and I feel terrible for all of those innocent people who were killed and for families who lost loved ones. It

138

doesn't matter what the reason was, whether it being that we don't practice the same religion that Afghans, or because they envy us because they're a poorer country, there is no excuse for the tragic crime the terrorists committed on that September day.

By:
Stephanie
Pfeffer

September 11th 2001

By: Hailee Parks (age 11)

I think what happened on September 11th 2001 happened because terrorists feel bad about themselves, their homes, and their country. Our nation is about the strongest nation that has ever fought for freedom.

Something that happened to our nation will be regreted. Our nation will stand tall, stand proud, and fight for what is right. I think terrorists of September 11th felt really bad about themselves to risk their life for a stupid reason their country will regret.

I think the war is almost over. Our country has almost defeated. Afghanastan is a bad country for not giving everybody equal rights. Everybody in Afghastan needs education, food, shelter, and most of all freedom.

I think that if we did become friends with them we should trade goods and be good to them.

Hailee

September 11TH 2001

I think what happened on September 11TH 2001 happened because terrorists feel bad about themselves, their homes, and their country. Our nation is about the strongest nation that has ever fought for freedom. Something that happened to our nation will be regreted. Our nation will stand tall, stand proud, and fight for what is right. I think terrorists of September 11TH felt really bad about themselves to risk their life for a stupid reason their country will regret. I think the war is almost over. Our country has almost defeated. Afghanistan is a bad country for not giving everybody equal rights. Everybody in Afghanstan needs education, food, shelter, and most of all freedom. I think that if we did become friends with them we should trade goods and be good to them.

Erica Craigston

Fallen Heroes

By: Shea Mahaffy (5th grade)

If you could speak to the families of the firefighters, policemen, and medical workers who died September 11th, what would you say to help them through this difficult time?

I would say that Ben Laden is a jerk. He did it for the stupidest reasons. The firefighters & policemen & medical workers did a job to save other peoples lives. They stood up for their nation & did their job, Because they are for others & you should be proud of them that they stood up for the nation & did their job to save others. So if you care a lot then make sure everyday you try to help others for their sake. Everytime you think of them then just remember the good times & that they were Brave.

Don't be afraid to have a good life even though they are gone. Because you will see them soon. They will be happy if you have a good life or they might be angry with themselves that you just gave up on your life for them. Even though they might feel that you love them a lot. You should make your life wild for them. Just never forget what happened on that day because life was hard then & it still can be. But be proud of what they did for their nation. It was a brave & bold thing they did.

Not everyone can be as brave & Bold to save people from fire, dust, ash, & smoke. Life is a great thing & for them to risk it all. That is the coolest thing ever. You should envy them because it is a great thing that they did.

Firefighters, policemen, & medical workers are a forever friend.

Shea
Mahaffy

If you could speak to the families of the fire fighters, policemen & medical workers who died on Sept 11th, what would you say to help them through this difficult time?

I would say that Bin Laden is a jerk. He did it for the stupidest reason. The firefighters & policemen & medical workers did a job to save other peoples lives. They stood up for their nation & did their job. Because they care for others & you. Should be proud of them that they stood up for the nation & did their job to save others. So if you care a lot then make sure everyday you try to help others for their sake. Everytime you think of them then just remember the good times & that they were Brave.

Don't be afraid to have a good life even though they are gone. Because you will see them soon. They will be happy if you have a good life or they might be angry with themselves that you just gave up on your life for them. Even though they might feel that you love them a lot. You should make your life wild for them. Just never forget what happened on that day because life was hard then & it still can be. But be proud of what they did for their nation. It was a brave & bold thing they did.

Not everyone can be as brave & bold to save people from the fire, dust, ash & smoke. Life is a great thing & for them to risk it all. That is the coolest thing ever. →

145

You should envy them because it is a great
thing that they did

Firefighters, policemen & medical workers are a
forever friend.

Thanks For Your Courage

By: Samantha Enloe (age 12)

Dear Medical workers, fire fighters, and police officers,

I as a fifth grader, am happy and sad at the same time, because what our country has ben through. I just want to remind you that our nation is so thankful for your courage, even though you may not have saved many at all. But if you were not there more people may have died. So thanks for your courage.

More people lived than died. I am almost positive that the whole United States of America would probably thank you for what you have done. If I went to every house in the United States of America, everyone would probably say that they would like to thank you for your braveness and thoughtfullness in America! All the families of people still in the hospitals would love to meet you, and thank you for helping the hurt children, adults and seniors still in a hospital.

147

Erica Craigston

Sincerely,

Samantha Enloe

~ + Sam~

Dear medical workers, fire fighters, and police officers, I as a fifth grader am happy and sad at the same time, because what our country has been through I just want to remind you that our nation is so thankful for your courage, even though you may not have saved many at all. But if you were not there more people may have died. So thanks for your courage more people lived then died. I am almost positive that the whole United States of America would probably thank you for what you have done. If I went to every house in the United States of America. Everyone would probably say that they would like to thank you for your braveness and thoughtfullness in america! All the families of people still in the hospitals would love to meet you, and thank you for helping the hurt children, adults and seniors still in a hospital.

Sincerely,

Samantha Enloe

148

Dear Children

By: Michelle de Wet (age 11)

Dear Children,

I know the tragedy that has happened is very sad. It was one of the worst things that has happened in America.

I know lots of children have lost love ones. I know that it is very difficult for us. But don't worry because your loved ones happily went to a better place and are now watching over you.

We will make it through because we are a very strong country which is a very good thing. Lots of other countries would just give up and not try to make it through, even if we lost loved ones.

Your loved ones would be very proud of us because we are making it through. I'm sorry for those people whose lost ones are gone. Its very very sad, & very stressfull for us.

If you are scared don't worry just talk to someone & let it all out. We will make it through no matter what happens.

You might feel mad, but we are looking for those who did this & they will pay for it.

Sincerely,

Michelle De Wet

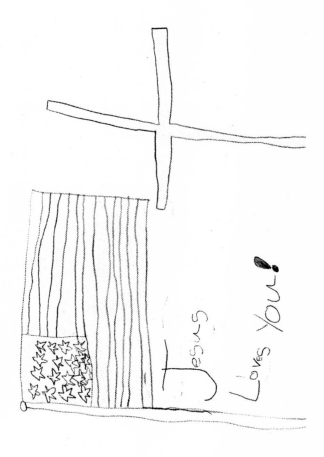

Tragedy in the U.S.A.

By: Brooke Brandt (age 11)

On September 11, 2001 there was a tragedy in the U.S.A. It was horrible because people died and were injured. Firefighters, policemen, and medical workers were just trying to save lives for others but some of them died with the others that were in it. America suffered that day but we stuck together through that tragedy and helped each other. Other countries are helping us with this tragedy because they respect us. It is not the country Afghanistan it is the terrorist camp.

People died and their family and friends were devastated and were full of sorrow and suffering. People ran for their lives from the Twin Towers. People felt sad even if they didn't have family and friends that died.

This tragedy will go in the history books forever. This tragedy was even worse than Pearl Harbor.

I can't believe that we, the U.S.A., let them come in our country.

Now our protection services is alot better and if anybody tries to get in and he is a terrorist he will be put in prison. I'm glad it has changed!

I can't believe that we, the U.S.A., let them come in our country.

Now our protection services is alot better and if anybody tries to get in and he is a terrorist he will be put in prison. I'm glad it has changed!

By,
Brooke
Brandt

9/11 /Essay

By: Christopher Mesger (age 11)

I think it all started when an Afghanistan person got on a plane and forced the driver to do what they wanted. I think the other Afghanistan people that were involved in the tragedy stole planes and were flying around. The first plane hit the World Trade Center and got blown up.

Then the other planes hit some other buildings. I think the Pilots of the plane were forced to crash into the buildings. If I was the pilot of a plane I would take it far away into a field and go straight into the ground, then the only people on that plane would die.

So that way I could help save our country. I would of prayed for the people that died and would help try to save our country. If I was a carpenter I would help build the World Trade Center back and the other buildings that we lost. I would of tried to stop the Afghanastans. There was a lot of people killed. I would of tried to save as many of the people as I can even if it killed me. Now we are in a war and I hope that we punish Bin Laden and we win the war. I just hope that no more of this happens again. Because if it does, where will they strike? They may kill you, me, and are families, and relatives.

Chris

I think it all started when an Afghanistan person got on a plane and forced the driver to do what they wanted. I think the other Afghanistan people that were involved in the tragedy. Stole planes and were flying around. The first plane hit the World Trade Center and got blown up. Then the other planes hit some other buildings. I think the pilots of the plane were forced to crash into the buildings. If I was the pilot of a plane I would take it far away into a field and go straight into the ground, then the only people on that plane would die.

So that way I could help save our country. I would of prayed for the people that died and would help try to save our country. If I was a carpenter I would help build the world Trade Center back and the other buildings that we lost. I would of tried to stop the Afghanastans. There was a lot of people killed. I would of tried to save as many of the people as I can even, if it killed me. Now we are in a war and I hope that we punish Bih Laden and we win the war. I just hope that no more of this happens again. because if it does, where will they strike? They may kill you, me, and our families, and relatives!

Erica Craigston

The newspaper photograph on the following page, taken by Diane Bondareff, shows two teenaged girls who lost their father in the World Trade Center attack. The teens are shown here holding a photo of their father as they prepared to attend the ceremony that marked the end of the recovery efforts at Ground Zero. The caption printed alongside this touching photo read:

Joanna Gomez, 13 and her twin sister Joanne hold a photo of their father Jose, who was a prep cook at Windows on the World restaurant at the World Trade Center, before attending the ceremony marking the end of the recovery effort at ground zero in New York, Thursday, May 30, 2002.

The photo is reprinted by permission of Associated Press.

The next section contains work contributed by teenagers. As I read their poignant words, I found myself dabbing the tears from my eyes as their reflections elicited strong feelings ranging from sadness to pride. Before 9/11, some people may have thought that today's younger generation didn't possess the patriotism shared by our forefathers. The works presented here as well as the actions and spirit of teens across America challenge that notion.

Immediately after the attacks teenagers reacted to the crisis by outfitting their vehicles, backpacks, and school books with American flags and stickers to show their patriotism. School halls across the nation were a blur of red, white, and blue as students used fashion to express their feelings of unity and allegiance. They proudly wore patriotic t-shirts, bandanas, pins, and hats. Teenagers willingly gave of their time and money helping with 9/11 causes wherever the opportunity arose. They flocked to chat rooms and discussion boards on Internet sites where they posted beautiful poems and offered their condolences through their compassionate words.

Erica Craigston

Five Minutes

By: Jarrett Barnes (age 17)

Forget your sleepers,

Forget your recruits,

They'll run and hide,

All the way to Beirut.

And hide they will try,

But to no avail,

Cause the U.S. Armed Forces

Are out to prevail.

I'm seventeen,

And I'll meet you soon,

Osama, just give me

Five minutes in a room.

Your sleepers aren't loyal,

They're brainwashed you see,

We'll fight till the end,

Just you and me.

It's freedom I fight for,

Not some caveman's cause,

But bring it on over,

We'll take you on.

If you're so brave,

Why must you run?

Just give me five minutes,

Your running will be done.

Your Jihad is over,

In five minutes time.

Come out of your cave,

Face a REAL soldier sometime.

Real soldiers stand tall,

U.S. Air Force, Marines.

Our Navy and Army,

They'll forever be seen!

So run if you want to,

And hide you may try.

In five minutes time,

You, too, shall die!

Cause the U.S. Armed Forces

Are coming you see!

In five minutes time,

You'll cease to be.

Dedicated to everyone in the U.S. Armed Forces...REAL soldiers!

Nine One One

By: Gina Tundley (age 15)

You're in my heart,

I know you're in pain.

Why'd this war start?

There's nothing to gain.

We lost great lives

On nine one one.

We can't undo

What's just been done.

I wish we could,

I'd give my all,

To bring back peace,

To one and all.

Erica Craigston

But please know this,

As you go on your way

We'll pray for you

Each and every day.

Dedicated to all 9/11 victims

Racial Profiling

By: Anthony Brown (age 17)

We have limited control over what other countries do. Sure, we have our treaties and summits. Our president meets theirs. But, when the handshakes are over and the signing is done, we still have no guarantees. Wouldn't you agree?

Since we have no guarantees, we have to be careful…both across the oceans and inside our borders. The problem is that we can't be careful without awakening the baby. The baby wakes up, crying and screaming, "Racial profiling, racial profiling! Quick, someone call a lawyer."

Look, I'm a teenaged African-American male. If anyone can empathize with the victims of discrimination, it's me. But, there's a big difference between discrimination and protection of all citizens. Your right to swing your fist stops where my face begins. If a person of Middle Eastern descent is thought to be acting suspiciously, doesn't this same concept hold true? Why should he have the right to kill the rest of us because we were too afraid of violating his civil rights to question him? We don't want to revert to the days when only white land-owning males had rights, but we need to be careful not to allow the pendulum to swing too far in the other direction.

Anyway, aren't we all victims of racial profiling? If I drive my beat-up Escort through the ritzy section of town, people will probably assume I'm up to no good. If my white friend John drives his dad's SUV into the projects, people will probably assume he's there to buy drugs. They'd be mistaken in both cases, but neither of us would call a lawyer over it.

We all have to sacrifice and put up with things we don't want to. It's part of living with others. At one time or another, we've all been "racially profiled." So what? We've lived to tell about it. So will they.

~*~ **My Beautiful Siggy** ~*~

Anonymous (teen)

a tribute to those we've lost...

a Swed, an Aussie, and two more Swedes......

also an African-Caucasian, altho we have only lost
her spiritually...

to Brian, to Ski, to Willsson and Marc......

to Reean...

always and forever

"Man's inhumanity to man makes countless
thousands mourn." <u>Robert Burns</u>

Erica Craigston

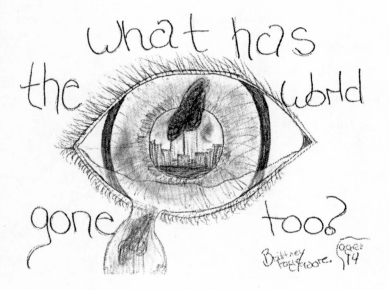

Mama

A song dedicated to the teenage girls who lost their moms on 9/11.

Anonymous

Mama, Mama, I'll miss you dearly.

You know I'll miss you.

Mama, Mama, why did you have to go?

Your love was for real, that I know.

Oh, Mama, Oh, Mama.

Mama, give me one more chance.

I'll put you far before romance.

So sorry I spoke those harsh words.

Wish I could take it back, how I wish, my lord.

Mama, Mama, I'll miss you dearly.

You know I'll miss you.

Mama, Mama, why did you have to go?

Your love was for real, that I know.

Oh, Mama, Oh, Mama.

Sorry I slammed the door, sorry I walked away.

This is too much to make a young girl pay.

Who'll wave to me as I walk down the aisle?

When I need you Mama, whose number do I dial?

Mama, Mama, I'll miss you dearly.

You know I'll miss you.

Mama, Mama, why did you have to go?

Your love was for real, that I know.

Oh, Mama, Oh, Mama.

I'll make you proud, just come back to me.

I know you'd do it, if God meant it to be.

Guess he had plans we don't understand.

Mama, I'm just not sure that I can.

Mama, Mama, I'll miss you dearly.

You know I'll miss you.

Mama, Mama, why did you have to go?

Your love was for real, that I know.

Oh, Mama, Oh, Mama.

I took you for granted, before nine-one-one.

I wish that I hadn't, but now it's all done.

Too late to go back, but I hope you know.

I'll love you forever, wherever you go

Mama, Mama, I'll miss you dearly.

You know I'll miss you.

Mama, Mama, why did you have to go?

Your love was for real, that I know.

Oh, Mama, Oh, Mama.

Erica Craigston

The following is a poem written by a friend of mine. He wrote this as he waited for his mother to come out of surgery. I included it here because it fits so appropriately with the previous song.

A Mother's Love…

A Mother's love is an instinctive love
Rarer and more precious than the most brilliant diamond
A unique love that only mothers alone can share
A love like no one could every have loved before
and a love no one will love in the same way afterwards

A Child's Love…

A Child's love is a deep-seated love
Rarer and more beautiful than a tender song
A peerless love that only a child alone can share
A love like no one could every have loved before
and a lasting love in the same way afterwards

174

Something to Think About

By: Ryan Wright (age 18)

Who said, "There are no atheists in foxholes?" Of course there are! To say that there aren't says that we think our belief system is stronger than that of an atheist. Pretty assuming of us. That's something to think about.

What happened to freedom of religion? Doesn't that include the freedom to disbelieve in religion? If not, then we've put ourselves on the same level as the Taliban members who believe Christians and Jews should be killed. That's something to think about.

If we enjoy freedom of religion and separation of church and state, as our government claims, then why were a group of atheists denied access to Ground Zero while a Christian group was allowed in? That's something to think about.

I'm a Christian, and I welcome one and all to my church, but I also respect your right not to believe in God. If we don't hold to this fundamental principle, then we are not truly free. That's something to think about.

Don't Blame Religion

By: Paul Bates (age 14)

What is this violence,
That comes from within?
I don't know, I can't know,
It must be pure sin.

You claim to be righteous,
A Jihad you say,
For an egotistical maniac
Who must have his way.

'Tis not Allah's wishes,
I don't believe it's true.
The God of real Muslims,
This He'd never do.

So don't blame religion,
For killing day after day.
For God wouldn't want this,
No how, no way.

Erica Craigston

Fallen

Anonymous (teen)

One day,

an ordinary day,

but every thing suddenly changes,

two towers fall,

some lose their all,

and nothing can be the same.

"You can only protect your liberties in this world by protecting the other man's freedom. You can only be free if I am free." Clarence S. Darrow

Fake

Anonymous (age 16)

I sat on my steps and cried a tear today for people I don't know.

When the kid next door cut me a look, I wiped my eyes and smiled and waved.

I felt like a fake, and then I cried some more, as I wondered if the children who lost their parents today would feel fakey as they made their way through life, pretending it's ok that their parents are gone.

I lost my parents when I was three, and that's how I feel...fakey...as I smile at my new foster parents, knowing they'll soon ship me off because I am "troubled."

But then I smiled, because I pretended all those kids had families who would take them in. I hope this is true and not just another figment of my imagination. The line between fake and real blurred long ago.

May God bless all the children who lost parents on 9/11. Know this children: You will survive and be strong.

The Nine Eleven Impact

By: Meagan Cane (age 17)

Nine eleven has made me grow up a little bit. I think it changed everyone in one way or the other.

My friends and I didn't think nine eleven directly affected us until one of our teachers put us in small groups. She asked us to make a list of changes/possible future changes that have/may occur because of nine eleven. Here's what we came up with:

— Other nations will become our allies because they will feel that if it could happen in the United States, it could happen anywhere.

— Other countries will ask us for more monetary and military assistance in exchange for their support.

— The United States may look at stricter immigration policies.

— There will be tighter security in public places.

— We will pay higher taxes to pay for the debt we will incur fighting terrorism at home and abroad.

— We will be forced to accept the loss of American soldiers because of the war on terrorism.

— We will get more cooperation from other countries to help us track possible terrorists.

— There will be increased job opportunities in Intelligence and security jobs.

— Developing closer ties to other countries may lead to improvements in education, health care, and housing for poorer nations.

— Some people in the United States may decide to move away from big cities.

— The travel industry may suffer.

— We will lose more civilian lives to future terrorists attacks.

Then, she asked each student to expand upon two items, telling exactly how it may impact his or her personal life. I chose immigration and job opportunities.

I feel that we may review our immigration policy and make some needed changes. If we had stricter immigration laws, I feel my future would be safer. We could still welcome others into our country, but we could maintain better control and know the immigrants whereabouts, especially if they are from a country that has links to terrorists' networks.

Before nine eleven, I thought I would become a paralegal, like my aunt. Now, I've changed my mind. I want to work for the CIA, so I can help track down terrorists before they are able to hurt anyone. So, I guess 9/11 pointed me toward my career choice.

Now, my friends and I realize that nine eleven affected everyone's future.

No Place Left to Run

By: Kasey (age 14)

There's no place left to run

You tried to tear our country apart,
You tried to break us down;
You took our brothers and sisters,
And you put them in the ground.

You used our planes against us,
Our people trapped inside;
You brought about destruction,
You crumbled America's pride.

You took our lovely buildings,
And you burnt them to the ground;
You terrorized our country,
Your hatred knew no bounds.

But now we're back and stronger then ever,
Together, "united as one;"

To put an end to terrorism,

Like the senseless acts you've done.

United, we are coming,

You had better load your guns;

America is after you,

There's no place left to run.

Sisters!

By: LaTonya Nighlander (age 17)

My father died two years ago and, because he was an organ donor, another person lived. I don't understand why my dad had to die, but I try to remember that his death gave someone else a chance to live. Dad would've wanted me to look for the positive side of our tragic loss.

In much the same way, I remember our Sisters in Afghanistan as we near the anniversary of 9/11. Until a few months ago, the Afghan women were forced to wear masks to cover their faces, and their ignorance was assured by the deprivation of an education.

Stand Proud, Sisters! Women Everywhere Unite! For it has not been so long ago that women like Florence Nightingale and Susan B. Anthony fought against repression in our country, so that you, my Sister, could be educated and free!

"To strive, to seek, to find, and not to yield."

Alfred Lord Tennyson

I Wonder

By: Elizabeth Downs (age 16)

The lilies in my yard bloom for the fifth year, and I wonder how many times I've walked by them without noticing.

I wonder how many times I have failed to breathe in their sweet, floral fragrance, to caress their soft petals between my fingers, or to detect the variation in shades amongst the colored beauties.

I wonder how many times I've walked out the door without telling my mother good-bye, or hugging my father's neck, as I know he likes.

I wonder how many times my little sister has asked me to read her a story, to which I sharply replied, "later," or, worse yet, pretended not to hear the squeaky pre-schooler's plea.

We have opportunities every day that thousands of people lost in a split second on Black Tuesday. I wonder how many more must die before we realize how precious our lives really are.

I See

Tizzy (age 17)

I used to see a tiresome old man sitting on the steps of our apartment building glaring at me as I talked to the boys on the corner who invited me into their cars, his eyes daring me to step in.

I used to see a janitor, slinging a mop bucket, back-and-forth, back-and-forth, and I wondered how anyone could stoop so low as to scrub toilets upon which others had sat.

I used to see a skinny man who watched me suspiciously, and I hated that he trusted me so little that he'd follow me to my basketball games.

Then, my friend's father died on Flight 77 on September 11th.

Now, I see my dad spending his evening outside on the steps of our apartment building to make sure I don't leave with some crazy boy, even though I know he'd rather watch television or rest after a long day at work.

Now, I see a man who works hard every day to provide money for me to have a better life, and to save money for my college, so I won't have to scrub toilets and mop floors.

Now, I see a proud father, who goes to work at 5am, so he can leave an hour early to watch his daughter play basketball.

If your parents are still with you, be thankful. My friend's father is gone, and I am proud that she could see him the way he really was before he died. Don't miss the opportunity to love others, because it could quickly be taken away.

Daddy, thanks for being patient until I learned to see.

Even Death Cannot Wash Them Clean

By: Mike Ford (age 17)

There is so much blood on the hands of the terrorists. Even death cannot wash them clean.

They thirst for more American blood, as if their throats were parched, yet their insides are gutless, while their hearts are full of hate.

Hate is a systemic poison that soon will seep out through their aortas and into every last cell in their bodies.

This raging hatred will bring more death and will blood-drench the hands of more terrorists. Even death cannot wash them clean.

It has been this way since the beginning of time, man against man, brother against brother, all in the name of religion. Actions of hatred, in the name of love. Even death cannot wash them clean.

Tombs and Children

By: Bobby Kennedy (age 18)

The newspaper is waiting. The room is still; the only signs of life in the immediate area are my footsteps advancing up the basement steps. Still only partially awake after my morning shower, I prepare my tea and take up the paper. The cover story is now familiar. Terrorists have crashed jet liners into the World Trade Center and Pentagon, and the first pages scream rage and disbelief in every headline. Each article is worded less like reporting and more like propaganda. I sigh and quickly flip through these, numb from two days of constant bombardment with shocking images and crumbling dreams. After a while the inescapable barrage of atrocity takes its toll on one's empathy. I return to the front pages, hoping for any differentiation from the expected. As I turn the page, a portrait greets my tired eyes, and they begin to open wide.

News cameras have caught a solitary man, in desperation leaping from the upper levels of the blazing World Trade Center, evidently praying for gravity's deliverance from humanity's flames. This man hangs there, caught forever between the life he once lived and the death that now looms before him.

The tragic stranger is not himself impressive, a simple white button down shirt, black slacks and a red tie, and yet his demise represents the sheer base nature of humanity, our own capacity for cruelty. That man could've been any average Joe in the United States, and yet when I see him hanging upside down, flailing with his last ounce of strength, reaching out to a better world, suddenly I know what humankind is like. No species on the planet can compare to the evil that is *Homo Sapiens*. People have killed each other for millennia, turning themselves and those around them into statistics I read about in history books. But the man, suspended forever in ink, is no number. His fate is our own despicable character screaming at us.

Newly depressed, and tired of the newspaper, I turn the page, deciding to put down the incriminating truth. Two steps through the door to the dining room, another photo catches my weary eye. Glasses, short, stark white hair and kind eyes smile at me from a picture of my grandmother, now deceased. No force of nature, be it storm or Parkinson's disease, could befoul her universal gentleness. Her compassionate words ooze through my sore mind, salving every aching neuron, and salvaging within me some hope for my species. Cookies, coffee, and carefully orchestrated morning cacophony dance along my brain, and I realize human nature is not a graveyard, but a city. Tombs compete with children playing in the streets of our being, and we decide unconsciously to which will be devoted our time. Kindness repelling the force of gravity.

Freedom is Not Free

By: Jim Hargrove (age 17)

We watch the news and see that we are at war, yet we do not fully comprehend.

We go about our lives (school, work, movies, friends). Never thinking about the soldiers risking their lives, so that we may go about carefree.

Let's stop and thank them, though words seem mundane. We see it on t-shirts and bumper stickers, but let's pause and fully comprehend the words:

FREEDOM IS NOT FREE

Only then can we pay them the respect they deserve. Only then can we appreciate our freedom.

Dedicated to my brother who serves in the U.S. Army, and all US soldiers, past, present, and future.

A Strong Nation

By: Emily Frost (age 14)

fear

sadness, sorrow

what if… again tomorrow?

anger

fear, dread

mixed emotions in my head

questions

with no answers

same sad song, second story

hope

love, compassion

USA

a strong nation

Tragedy

By: Clarissa Whitfield (age 18)

Our loved ones gone
With no tomorrow
People's hearts
Full of sorrow

Mourning for families
Longing for friends
Wondering if someday
The tragedy might end

Full of heartache
Full of pain
Everything lost
Nothing more to gain

All on a day
A day no one can bare
September Eleventh
A day of horrible scare

No Longer Enough

By: James Ratcliff (age 17)

It is obvious after 9/11 that our military strength and economic power is no longer enough to keep Americans safe. I think we will have to develop improved intelligence, security, and foreign relations, as well as cooperation among government agencies.

Just as a football team reviews their games on tape to discover what they could've done better, so must the government review policies and find out where our intelligence system failed prior to 9/11. It is difficult to believe, given today's technology, that we couldn't have tracked the terrorists' activities prior to the tragedy. We have to be able to track a foreigner who is supposed to be a student, yet isn't going to college, but is, instead, training to be a pilot!

Our security has improved since 9/11, but we still have a long way to go. Recently, I saw on the news where people got through airport security with unauthorized items. And nearly a year has passed since 9/11! We have to move quicker on this issue if we want to be safe.

There needs to be improved communication between government agencies. Why were student visas issued for two dead terrorists six months after the attacks? We can't improve intelligence and security without improving communications.

We must continue to improve our relations with other countries. If our military superiority didn't stop terrorists on 9/11, then it won't necessarily keep us safe. Terrorists move freely from country to country. We have to depend on other countries to help us track them. These countries must trust and like us, or they will not help us.

I think the United States is working on all these areas. I hope we continue to pursue these goals to ensure our safety.

Today

By: Jody McCleary (age 15)

Today is 9/11/02.

Let us not forget.

Tomorrow, I may go to the movies with my boyfriend,

But today, I'll say a prayer for those still in pain.

Tomorrow, my girlfriends and I may shop for clothes,

But today, I'll light a candle in remembrance of others.

Tomorrow, I may ask my mom to help me with schoolwork,

But today, I'll hold vigil through the night for those who died.

Tomorrow, I'll ponder my career options,

But today, I'll thank emergency workers who sacrificed a year ago.

Today, I am reminding you,

But tomorrow, I will again.

Today is 9/11/02.

Let us not forget.

The Third Mile

Anonymous (age 17)

My dad runs marathons. Twenty-six miles. It takes months of training and a lot of discipline to get to the finish line. What would be the point of running if he was going to sit down at the three-mile marker?

That's where we are, America...the third mile. President Bush informed us early on that this war would not be quickly won, but that it would be a long, sustained effort. We all nodded and clapped, making noises we thought were expected. Why then, are some of us sitting down with twenty-three miles left to go?

Already, we are losing momentum on the home front. In September, a few days after the attacks, security checks for travelers were approved by 93% of Americans. Six months later, that figure declined four percent. E-mail and cell phone monitoring were acceptable to 54% of Americans right after the attacks, but in six months time, only 44% still remained supportive. These may not seem like huge numbers, but 10% is a lot considering we only had a little over half the people supporting the measure to begin with.

I'm not a blind follower, and I understand that we must keep a check on our civil liberties, but everything is give and take. I see my choices as this: Give the U.S. government some leeway, or give the terrorists an opportunity to take more American lives.

Since I'm not doing anything illegal, I don't imagine anyone would listen in on my cell phone too long. And what has it really hurt if a stranger hears me arguing with my girlfriend on my cell phone? (Which I doubt would ever happen...not the arguing, the eavesdropping...because no red flags would point authorities in my direction.) I couldn't care less if someone knows which books I checked out at the library, or which Internet sites I visited.

Grandma always says not to do anything you wouldn't want the preacher to know about. I try to live by that advice. Even if you don't want your preacher to know, unless you're planning to kill someone or commit some other serious crime, you probably don't have much to worry about. I'm more worried about another terrorist attack than I am about the government knowing that my grandma still calls me Babyface or that I read Garfield daily.

Yes, I understand about civil liberties, and I certainly don't want to lose my rights. But sometimes, it comes down to the lesser of two evils. Yes, I understand why there are people who don't particularly trust the government. But, if I must choose between trusting our government and trusting radical Muslims who hate us and will die to kill us, I will choose our government.

We are in the third mile, Americans. I urge each of us to look deep within ourselves and find the determination to finish the race. Quitters never win, and winners never quit. And we, fellow Americans, are winners!

Erica Craigston

Freedom is Not Free

By: Jenny Owensboro (age 16)

After the 9/11 attacks occurred, I heard a few people say, "We should blow the Middle East off the face of the earth." I'm ashamed to admit it, but that almost seemed like a good idea to me in the aftershock of our losses. But, after I thought about it, I decided that it's really not a good idea at all.

There are good people and bad people in the Middle East, just as there are in America. I'd no more want to harm innocent Arabs than Americans. If we did kill innocent civilians, wouldn't that make us just like the Taliban? That's what Osama bin Laden and his radical followers want— for us to be like them.

They hate us for our freedom, democracy, and human rights. If we cease to be humanitarians, then, surely, we will be no different from our enemy. We cannot only be humanitarians at home or when it suits our cause, any more than we can be Christians on Sunday and pagans on Saturday night. If we act in this manner, we are hypocrites. If we believe in human

204

rights at home, then we must believe in human rights in the Middle East.

Regardless of my belief in human rights, I must say it was difficult not to detest the Arabs when I saw them laughing, celebrating, and burning American flags on 9/11. But, think about the situation. The civilians there are terrified to speak out against the Taliban, so, if the Taliban was celebrating our loss, maybe they'd just go along with it out of fear. Also, I believe these people are brainwashed into believing we are evil.

It reminds me of when slaves were freed in the United States, and some of them decided to stay with their masters, even though they were legally free to go. They stayed because it was all they knew. That didn't make slavery a great thing. They simply didn't see that they had a choice. Maybe the Arab civilians don't feel they have a choice either.

If we kill civilians without regard for their human rights, then we will not have honored our civilians lost on 9/11. If we lose sight of the fact that we believe in human rights, then the terrorists have won.

Angel Wings

By: Sara Davidson (age 14)

As I looked at the clock,
While I laid in bed,
"Just another Tuesday,
Nothing special," I said.

Take the six o'clock train,
Everyday, on the dime,
No time for "Good mornings,"
Got to get there on time.

Then a big thud, a crash,
What's that I smell?
What? Before I know it,
The North Tower just fell.

We climbed to the roof,
And thought we'd be free,
But the door was locked,
It wasn't meant to be.

There's still time to get out,
I keep telling my friend,
But I know all along,
Our time is at its end.

I watched my friend jump,
And was no longer scared,
Cause angel wings took him,
There was no cross to bear.

So weep for yourselves,
But please not for me,
Cause soon your own angel
Will bring you, you'll see.

Together Again

Anonymous (age 13)

If you lost a loved one on 9/11, I am sure you are very hurt, and there is probably little I can say to help you, except maybe this:

I am 13 now but it seems like only yesterday that I was 6. My mom is 40 but she said it seems like only yesterday that she was my age. Time on earth passes quickly but you will have an eternity with your loved one in heaven. Even if you live to be 90, the time will pass quickly so you will see your loved one very soon.

My grandma died last year and I miss her. My mom said I should remember the good times and try to be happy because that's what grandma would have wanted. I think your loved one would feel the same way.

Until you are together again, I will pray for your happiness. The whole nation is praying for your happiness.

"Grieve not as those who have no hope." (1 Thessalonians 4:13)

I Remember

By: LaTreese Goldstein (age 15)

If I wake up in the morning and I don't want to go to school,

I remember the kids in villages that have no schools.

If I look in the mirror and worry that I'm five pounds too heavy,

I remember the refugees dying from malnutrition.

If I start to complain about curfews and driving laws,

I remember the countries that have no democracy.

If I wish my parents would leave me alone,

I remember those who lost their parents at the hands of terrorists.

Dedicated to all the kids who lost a parent on 9/11. We all mourn with you.

Taken in September

Anonymous (age 18)

The wind whispers through the trees,

And I think I hear your voice,

With it's thick Jersey accent,

Then I remember, you were taken in September.

I step on a crowded subway,

Where a gentleman offers me a seat,

And his kindness reminds me of you,

Then I remember, you were taken in September.

I catch a sideways glimpse of a smile,

And a hearty laugh soon follows,

And I turn, knowing it is you,

Then I remember, you were taken in September

A man shoulders against me on Fifth,

As he passes, I catch the scent of Cool Water,

And I turn to see if it is you,

Then I remember, you were taken in September.

Each day, everywhere I turn,

I feel the void in my life,

Though I fight it, the universe forces me

To remember you were taken in September

My prayer is that I won't be alone.

Though you may not have lost a loved one,

Please help me bear this load,

Let's remember those who were taken in September.

They Died So We Could Be Free

By: Jeanine McGraw (age 16)

They died so we could be free,
Even, if inadvertently.

They gave their lives as surely as soldiers,
Calling to say bye, what could've been bolder?

Who would've known we couldn't recover
A brother, a sister, or somebody's mother?

Their deaths brought us together to honor our flag,
Charlie Daniels said it best, "It's a flag, not a rag."

Their sacrifice united us quickly, you see,
And patriotism to the forefront, again shall be.
So definitely, they died so we could be free,
Even, alas, if inadvertently.

Day by Day

By: Nicole Everest (age 17)

When I dropped you at the airport,
Who'd have guessed it'd be,
The last time I'd see you,
Or your eyes would see me.

When I heard the news,
I kept steady, praying,
Survivors they would find,
But fate wasn't so kind.

"Life is for the living, Go on,"
They all say,
I'm trying, making progress,
Day by day.

All I can hold on to,
Is knowing what we shared,
Is more than some ever know,
Cause that's how much you cared.

Ever moving gently, carefully,

I'll trudge ahead so slow,

Till our God reunites us,

Forever and ever more.

And when that day comes,

So joyous it will be,

For I will have made it,

Daily for you and me.

Dedicated to all 9/11 victims. May God Bless you.

Erica Craigston

September 11th— How I See It

Chris Duncan (age 15)

What I can't understand about September 11th is how Osama bin Laden found enough sick people willing to help him carry out the attacks. What is even more confusing is that everyone in the Middle East seemed to be happy about it. The news showed footage of them partying, celebrating, and burning American flags. I believe these people need serious mental help.

Think about this: If you suggested to several Americans that they go crash planes into a building (or several buildings) in Afghanistan, chances are good that you wouldn't get any takers. If you *were* able to kill some Arabs, Americans wouldn't be partying in mass numbers— we would be horrified!

What is *wrong* with these people? How could this many mentally ill people be walking the streets? Our neighbors in the Middle Eastern countries need to invest in some serious mental health programs. And if they're not mentally ill, they must be very, very evil. I'm not sure which one is more dangerous.

I'm not writing this to insult anyone. This is simply how I see it.

Justice

By: April Crutchfield (age 16)

If I die because I crash my Mustang,
Please don't sue Ford.

If I drown at summer camp,
Please don't hold the lifeguard responsible.

If my young body is taken over by cancer,
Please accept that it was my time to go.

But, if I perish at the hands of a terrorist,
Please do not rest until you have avenged my
death.

We owe justice to our 9/11 victims.
Let's see that our debt is paid.

Thanks

By: Brandon Smith (age 17)

To the paramedics and EMT's who rushed to the scene on 9/11,
Thank you.

To the firefighters who ran into an inferno to try to save others,
Our gratitude runs deep.

To the police officers who responded to help where they could,
We are grateful.

To the construction clean-up crews who sifted through the carnage with heavy hearts,
We appreciate your willingness to help.

To everyone who contributed in any way,
The nation appreciates your sacrifice.

To the countries who have stood beside us,
We are forever in your debt.

Rest Now

By: Victoria Stonefield (age 16)

Rest now, ole Fire Chief.

While the rest of us are stricken with grief.

We mourn our loss,

yet, we know you died serving others, as was your
life.

So, rest now.

Rest now, New York Blue.

To America, you've paid your due.

You put up a fierce fight

to save the lives of strangers.

So, rest now.

Rest now, government servant.

In the Pentagon, you were doing our service.

Your life was meaningful,

and we appreciate your contribution.

So, rest now.

Rest now, everyday worker.

Our tears have flooded and are yet to be corked.

We miss you dearly,

and appreciate what you added to life.

So, rest now.

Rest now, dear traveler.

As we try to put back what has unraveled.

Your life was precious,

and your accomplishments noted.

So, rest now.

"The pain of the mind is worse than the pain of the body." <u>Publilius Syrus</u>

Mommy

By: Tina (teen)

My mommy got ready for work today,
Just like she always does.
She put on her skirt,
And her pretty white blouse,
And gave me a present,
"Just because."

Even though she'd be late,
She made me breakfast,
With bacon, eggs,
And heart shaped pancakes.

She blew me a kiss,
As she ran out the door,
She said, "Honey, I love you,
I'll be home before four!"

Daddy came to pick me up,
From my kindergarten class,

He was late,

But I still love him,

Even though I was picked up last.

Daddy waited a while with me,

Just like every day,

We always wait for mommy to come home,

But she seemed to be late today.

"When will mommy be coming home?"

"Will she be here soon?"

"Can I watch TV while I'm waiting dad?"

"Can I watch Cartoons?"

Daddy looked at me,

With his big brown eyes,

He said,

"No don't turn on the TV,

Lots of people are dead."

He sat me down right next to him,

On the big white chair,

He said, "Mommy and I both love you"
And he was playing with my hair.

Daddy asked me if I know the towers,
Where mommy goes every day,
And I told him of course I do,
She went there to work today.

Daddy looked so sad right then,
He looked like he was going to cry,
He told me bad men took over a plane,
And crashed it,
And my mommy died.

He said I'd never see her again,
But she was in a better place,
He said she'll still be with us,
Even though I can't see her face.

"Why did they take her away from me?
She didn't do anything wrong,
She shouldn't be in heaven yet daddy,

Home is where she belongs!"

As I ran up to my room,
I heard my daddy say,
"Baby, Don't cry,
Mommy will be ok!"

At the funeral,
For my mommy dear,
I held my daddy's hand,
While scary people came near.

Before they buried my mommy,
I went to her new bed,
Her new bed in the ground,
Because bad guys made her dead.

I put a teddy on her grave,
It was a special one, you know,
It was the one she gave me,
The morning she died,
And I screamed,

"Mommy please don't go!"

Bad guys took my mommy away,

For no reason at all,

They took lots of other mommy's and daddy's away,

Some are still buried in the walls.

Now it's just daddy and me,

Now we're all alone,

I really miss my mommy,

Mommy please come home.

Holy War

By: David P. (age 18)

Does anyone else find the term holy war ironic? There is nothing holy about war. I realize that wars have been fought since biblical times, but that doesn't make war holy.

Is this war necessary? Now that terrorists have initiated it, yes, it is very necessary. But, here's the sad truth— U.S. soldiers will die in this war and the entire war could've been avoided. That's right, avoided.

How? By closing off our borders to Middle Eastern nations. I am not a racist, but we cannot trust these people. If we hadn't let them in, 9/11 wouldn't have happened, and we wouldn't be fighting an almost impossible enemy who flees from country to country undercover. Notice, I didn't say totally impossible...just almost impossible. We will win, but what a shame we didn't avoid it.

You say we need these countries for their oil? Ha! I don't believe it. The United States must have the technology to create an alternative fuel. Think about all the technological advances we've made over the last ten years…it has to be possible to find a way around our dependence on oil from countries that hate us. It simply has to be in the best interests of the right people— people with power and money. Until it is in the interest of these select people, an alternative fuel will never be developed.

You say it is anti-American to deny a group of people access to our country? If you were forced to make a decision between burning to death and jumping 100 stories to the concrete below, you may reconsider your position. Face it…whether we like it or not, these people absolutely hate Americans. Sure, there may be a few good ones, but why should we risk our lives trying to find those few and far between good apples when most of the barrel is so rotten it stinks?

So, have your war. But don't call it holy. There is nothing holy about war.

9-11 Essay

By: Courtney Bridges (age 14)

I remember that when I first heard about the first plane hitting the World Trade Center I was in math class. An announcement came over the PA system. Our principal made the announcement and she sounded like she was about to cry. Everyone got very quiet. My teacher Mrs. Dexter turned on the TV so we could watch the news.

The whole day seemed like a dream. In the hallways, no one was laughing or cutting up. Everyone was kind of quiet. I can never remember our hallways being quiet at any other time since I have been in school. It was totally strange.

A couple of my friends were upset because they had relatives who worked in Manhattan, but they weren't sure exactly where. Later, they found out their relatives were not harmed so they felt better. But they didn't find this out until late that night or maybe the next day, so they felt terrible all day. We felt bad for them, but we didn't really know what to say to them, so we just kept saying that we were sure their relatives would be fine and to try not to worry so much about it.

Over the next few weeks, I learned a lot about the Middle East and terrorism. I also learned that a lot of other countries like Canada are very sympathetic about what happened to the United States. My dad said that even some of the countries that might not like us that much are still on our side anyway. Maybe they are afraid that Osama bin Laden will come after them and they will have to ask us to help them because we have a very strong military force.

I am still kind of afraid because the terrorists could strike again and kill all of us. I hope our soldiers and President Bush make sure this doesn't happen again. I have a lot of faith in our soldiers and in our president. If President Bush ran for president again after I turned eighteen, I would vote for him because I think he has done a good job handling the 9-11 crisis. I think most people would panic and not know what to do, but he has been able to stay calm and do whatever he had to do to help our country. I always watch him on television, and I think he really cares about the victims.

If I were older I would join the navy, too, because I want to do something to help our country. I think a lot of kids my age feel that way. My boyfriend said he would like to become a soldier so he can go pull the terrorists out of the caves. I don't want to do that, but maybe I could learn to operate some of the computers on a navy ship. This would be a good way to serve my country.

Home

By: Jordan Lancaster (age 15)

In this life you always soared,

But now on earth, you exist no more.

I bet in heaven your wings do shine,

I hope one pair you've saved as mine.

Soon the Pearly Gates shall open wide,

Your family can't wait to come inside.

Until that day, we'll patiently wait,

This I promise, I won't be late.

When God calls me Home,

I won't be alone.

You've been with the Son

Since nine-one-one.

"The God who gave us life gave us liberty at the same time."

Thomas Jefferson

Erica Craigston

The Good Old Days

Anonymous (age 16)

I awoke this morning, wondering if today
would be another September 11th,
And if it is, where will it occur?
North, South, East, or West?

I attend my high school's football game
and I suspiciously eye two men speaking
in a foreign tongue.
Are they strapped with explosives?

I wanted to go to Six Flags with my friends today
but I've heard that large crowds
make likely terrorists targets.
Will it happen today?

Life was simpler before September 11th.
That's what my generation will mean
when we say The Good Old Days.

Yet, I know I must overcome my fears
and carry on.
I'll have to do it a little at a time
until I feel safer.

Time and Love

By: Melanie Brooks (age 17)

Though you will never forget your loved one,
You will one day be able to smell the flowers again.
Time and love will ease your wounds.

Though you will always hold your loved one dear,
Someday, you will again enjoy a sunset.
Time and love will ease your wounds.

Though your loved one will remain in your heart,
You will eventually relish a walk on the beach, as you smell the salty ocean breeze.
Time and love will ease your wounds.

Though each year, the date September 11 will linger as a terrible reminder,
Time and love will ease your wounds.

To My Friend

By: Missy W. (age 15)

It's been nearly a year since the 9/11 attacks, but I have not forgotten your pain. I see it in your eyes and in the way you move— no longer with purpose and joy, but as if each step were an effort.

Before 9/11, you were such a cheerful friend. Now, understandably, you lack the carefree attitude that made you...well, you, and it saddens me to the core of my heart. You used to talk and laugh and be the life of the party. Now, you are distant. I want to be the friend I think you need, but I don't know how any more. I've done everything I can think of, but nothing seems to cheer you up. I am at a loss.

You lost your father on 9/11, and, in a way, I lost my best friend. I am not comparing my loss to yours, because at least you are still here. I want things to go back to the way they were before, though I don't know if they ever will.

I feel bad for feeling this way, because I know it sounds racist, but every time I see a Middle Easterner,

I want them to leave our country. I am afraid of them, and they remind me of the reason for the sadness in your eyes.

I wish for the joy to return to your life. Maybe I am selfish, but I also wish for my best friend to come back to me. I miss her. I watch us slip further apart each day, but I don't know how to stop it.

Dedicated to everyone who lost a friend or relative to 9/11, directly or indirectly.

Borders

Anonymous (age 18)

Many generations ago, people flocked to the United States for a better life. That's all they wanted...an opportunity for a happier, healthier, wealthier life. They didn't want to come over here to kill Americans.

Many generations ago, there wasn't high unemployment funded by working Americans. It wasn't like foreigners were coming in and taking over American jobs, pushing those people into the unemployment line, or worse yet, into a life of crime. (People who need money are more likely to commit crimes. No job = no money = desperation = crime).

Many generations ago, we had room for more people and no reason to fear them, so, it was fine that the United States allowed them in. Times have changed and we need to scale back our immigration. Or, better yet, close the borders off completely to people from nations we know hate Americans. We have all the people here we can handle, and we can't trust the foreigners from these American-hating nations.

This whole, "land of the free" thing is overstated anyway. We can't be free until we get all these foreigners who want to kill us out of the US. We're all waiting on the next sleeper cell to awaken and start the killing again. That is not what I call free. So, where's the free in land of the free?

If a man broke into your house, would you wait until he started killing your family before you shot him? I wouldn't. I'd get rid of him the minute he walked in the door. But we're not doing that. We're going to sit here and wait until he starts killing. This dishonors the 9/11 victims!

Miss You

By: Christy Rodgers (age 13)

When God called your name,
I wasn't ready for you to go.
Still, you went ahead,
And now I miss you so.

What's heaven like?
I bet it's beautiful up there.
I know you make the angels smile,
As you made your friends down here.

But not to worry; don't despair,
I'll be with you someday.
I've missed you so since 9/11,
When a terrorist took you away.

I'll be good and pray each night,
And serve throughout my life.
I'll be repaid when we reunite,
But till then, I'll miss you each day.

Ground Zero Cleanup

By: Brett Thompson (age 18)

My father is in business for himself, and he sometimes takes jobs cleaning up after construction crews, or doing fire and water damage restoration. Because I've been around this business all my life, I'm very aware of what the cleanup workers went through at Ground Zero.

The crews cleaning up at Ground Zero had a tough job. It had to be depressing to dig through the rubble where so many innocent lives were taken out of pure hate for Americans.

I think many people have overlooked these workers, and they may feel that America doesn't understand what they went through. When I was given an opportunity to write an essay for this book, I knew it would be to say thank you to these workers.

Ground Zero Cleanup Crew: Even if we haven't expressed it, we realize how difficult your jobs were, and we appreciate your service. Sorry you had to view such horrendous loss day after day. Someone had to do it, and you stepped up to the plate. So, thank you for your service. This was not just another job.

Erica Craigston

Outsider

Anonymous (age 15)

My brother and I fight a lot, but neither of us lets anyone else pick on the other one. I may call my brother a name or tell on him to get him in trouble, but if anyone else tries to hurt him, they'll have to go through me first. If an outsider picks on one of us, it only pulls us closer together.

That's all Osama bin Laden has done...pulled us closer together. We may argue among ourselves, but we won't have an outsider pushing us around. The sooner Caveman learns this, the better off he'll be!

Osama, you found 19 morons to die for your cause. Well, now you have millions of us to deal with. Don't send another fool. Be brave enough to come over here yourself! You started it, now face it!

Trust Our Government

By: Ericka N. (age 16)

Lady Liberty is blindfolded.

I think it was meant to represent no discrimination here (in the US). It will be difficult, but I know we can keep it that way and still protect ourselves from terrorists.

I am not perfect, but I try to be as good of a teenager as I can for my parents. My parents make mistakes, but I know I can trust them to do their best. This is how I feel about our government protecting us. I'm sure they made mistakes, but I still trust the government to do the best they can to make sure another attack like 9/11 doesn't ever happen again.

Remembrance and Freedom

Anonymous (teen)

The moment I heard
I didn't feel scared,
But there was something inside me
I just couldn't bare

It felt like a yearning,
something I need to do.
There were so many out there,
who had pain to suffer through

And all I could do,
was watch the news and wonder why,
someone could do this sort of thing
and I let out a cry

People took away life
trying to make their stand,
but our nation stuck together
everyone lent a hand.

But it hurt me to know

thousands more would die.

We were off to Afghanistan

With the blink of an Eye

The ignorance of our nation

Started to show

though people thought they saw

the Patriotism show

Our country stands

For freedom and peace.

And we didn't show our nation's greatness

when we invaded the Middle East.

For Ghandi put it well,

and through love we could find

"An Eye for an Eye

Makes the world go blind"

Fighting for peace

Makes no sense to me

Peace means no war

Everyone is free

So while we fight this war

and search for just one

Remember what we stand for

and that this war brings peace to none.

Pulling Together

By: T.H. (age 17)

Democracy doesn't just happen.
It demands effort of each of us,
It takes the teamwork of a nation,
Pulling together, never apart.

The war on terrorism won't be won by soldiers alone.
It will take the support of each of us,
In and out of uniforms,
Pulling together, never apart.

Hearts broken on 9/11 will not mend by themselves.
It will take the prayers of many,
Each of us, in prayer,
Pulling together, never apart.

I Am American, I Am Proud
By: Felicia (age 14)

I remember exactly where I was and exactly what I was doing on September 11, 2001. I was in Social Studies class, coming up with reasons about why Maine was special, why Hope was special, and why America was special. A special education teacher came in, and only told us that two planes had crashed, and where. That is all we knew.

You can understand why we were confused when the school secretary came in and told my friend that her mother didn't want her at soccer practice. I went home, and my Mom had on the TV. I just stood there in front of the TV, frozen by the horrible images before my eyes. They kept doing a replay of the plane hitting the buildings...it was terrible. I got online, to talk to my friends. We were always talking about being bored out of our minds, and why couldn't Hope be more interesting. (Hope is where I live.) We never wanted or expected anything like this to happen.

In school the next day, it was all people could talk about. What they had seen, the people actually jumping to their deaths to avoid being burned alive, or smothered. It was terrible. I didn't know any of the people that had been hurt in the accident, but it effected me in such a large way. My whole school, which is about 160 students, went to the gym to sing patriotic songs. We were singing America the Beautiful, and my friend Heather was standing there, singing her heart out with tears streaming down her face. I started crying as well, and I put my arm around her. On the Friday, when you were supposed to light a candle outside, I went to my friend Jessie's with Marianne. We didn't just light a candle; we had a bonfire. Everyone that passed saw us— we weren't only doing it for fun— we were doing it to show everyone you couldn't bring us down. You can't kill the spirit of America.

Even now I am still effected by the events of September 11, 2001, isn't everyone? That day will never be forgotten, it will go into history books. September 11 was the day when terrorists tried to tear us down, take away the spirit that each and every American has. I hope it has now occurred to everyone, that you can't take our spirit. Anything you do to tear us down only makes us stronger. I am Felicia. I am an American. I am proud.

Show Me

By: Tiffany Knight (age 17)

Show me a country stronger than ours.
There isn't one.

Show me a more united front than America's.
One has never existed.

Show me a flag more beautiful than the Stars and
Stripes.
Your eyes will never gaze at one.

Show me braver soldiers than those who wear the
U.S. emblem upon their sleeves.
Others run and hide in caves while our men and
women face the fight.

Show me a gift more priceless than freedom.
It is forever unseen, for it doesn't exist.

Show me a country whose people will never stop praying for our 9/11 victims.

Ahh, that is America. Land of the Free, Home of the Brave!

.. /#@?!*Jesus said these words*!?@#/..

By: Brittney Faye Moore (age 14)

I am the light, he who follows me
will never be in the darkness.

I LOVE YOU, JESUS CHRIST!
9/11/01
Tuesday, I was in my electronics
class and I was watching TV(News)
when I saw the first airplane
hit one of the towers I thought
that it was an accident, then
when I saw the second one
hit then I knew that
we (AMERICA) were in trouble.
Later on in class I saw the pentagon with
all of those flames, and then
I already knew that we (AMERICA)
were going to be at war for
JUSTICE!

Erica Craigston

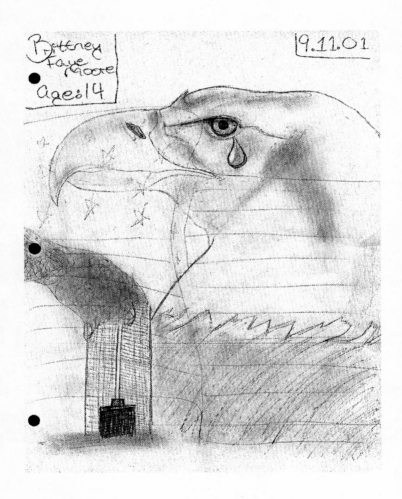

Wounds

By: Harmony McDowell. (age 17)

Deep wounds are difficult to heal,
And 9/11 is the deepest cut we've seen,
So we step back and allow you time to grieve.

And we will grieve beside you on bended knee,
With our hands extended to pull you up,
But, not until you are ready to arise and step forward with life.

Take the time you need, but know that we are here for you,
When you're ready to move on, never forgetting, always honoring,
And living the full life your lost love would have wanted.

Until then, we will grieve beside you on bended knee,
With our hands extended to pull you up.

How Can I Help?

By: Tina (teen)

What do you do,

When there's nothing you can do?

What do you say,

When there's nothing you can say?

A million miles away,

Scared to death of the world itself,

Feeling helpless and hopeless,

All of sanity,

Just fell off its shelf.

You want to do something,

To help the unhelped,

You want to say something,

To relieve what is felt.

What do you do,

When all you do doesn't help,

What do you say,

When you want to make everything,

Better today.

stereotypical

Anonymous (age 15)

this life is full of technicalities

and skid marks that can't be erased

it seems we've all been though a copy machine

and given a specific time and place

in the end, we all have the same color of hair

we all want the exact same thing

pleasure and money, our biggest concerns

turn out for the worst, yet nothing is changed.

stereotypical minds walk the streets

knowing it's a contradiction

controversial issues ruin

all hope for elimination

recycled phrases pass

between shallow minds

eagle eyes are watching, searching

for respect they'll never find.

the ground below us is crumbling

and on it more houses are built

all of the same make and color

like a huge designer quilt

the rolling hills are replaced with mansions

riches turned to rags

we promise to bond together now

but are forced to wear name tags.

and the alarm clock sounds, we're up again

with no money back guarantee

we take another cosmopolitan quiz

and swallow another key

we cage another one of our kind

without a second thought

pretending things are all okay

but knowing too well they're not.

we have hair curlers and cd burners

policemen and medicine men

cloning techniques mixed with hatred

mistakes again and again

there are guns in the hands of children

bloodsheed much too near

there are metal detectors in our schools

and we're told there is nothing to fear.

Photos similar to the one on the following page held the country captive as we tried to comprehend the horrendous events of September 11th. This photograph, taken by Carmen Taylor, was accompanied by the following caption:

A jet airliner is lined up on one of the World Trade Center towers in New York Tuesday, Sept. 11, 2001. In the most devastating terrorist onslaughts ever waged against the United States, knife-wielding hijackers crashed two airliners into the World Trade Center on Tuesday, toppling its twin 110-story towers.

The photo is reprinted by permission of Associated Press.

I wish to extend my deepest gratitude to everyone who contributed work to this book. Some students opted to remain anonymous. I hope I have included the name of everyone who wished to be listed. If I have omitted anyone, please accept my apologies, and know that your work is deeply appreciated along with the writings and artwork of those who requested anonymity.

Following are the names of many young authors and artists whose work made this project a reality:

Jaclyn Bailey

Jarrett Barnes

Beau Bartolotta

Ted Barton

Paul Bates

Nick Batey

Erica Beckett

Brooke Brandt

Courtney Bridges

Dustin Britton

Melanie Brooks

Anthony Brown

Meagan Cane

April Crutchfield

Sara Davidson

Cody Davis

Michelle de Wet

Elizabeth Downs

Sam DuBois

Chris Duncan

Samantha Enloe

Nicole Everest

Mike Ford

Rose Freeman

Emily Frost

Suzie Givens

LaTreese Goldstein

Darian Haffer

Jim Hargrove

Derek Harris

Jen Hess

Amanda Higgs

Tiffany Knight

Jordan Lancaster

Amber Lindley

Marvin Lumos IV

Shea Mahaffy

Phillip McChesney

Jody McCleary

Ian McCoig

Harmony McDowell

Jeanine McGraw

Christopher Mesger

Brittney Faye Moore

LaTonya Nighlander

Ericka Nunley

Stephanie Nye

Maria Ortiz

Jenny Owensboro

Hailee Parks

Diane Preston

Stephanie Proffer

James Ratcliff

Hailey Reid

Erica Craigston

Dillon Renfro

Kelsey Richards

Kerry Roberts

Devon Robinson

Christy Rodgers

Brandon Smith

Amy Sparks

Victoria Stonefield

Katie Strauser

Brett Thompson

Gina Tundley

Clarissa Whitfield

Lydia Wilcox

Christopher Williams

Alex Witt

Ryan Wright

Bibliography

"A Rush of Volunteers Big Brothers Big Sisters Eyes Kids' Post— 9/11 Needs." <u>Daily News (New York)</u>. 14 Jan 2002, Sec.NEWS:26.

Applewhite, Ashton, Evans III, William, Frothingham, Andrew. (1992). <u>And I Quote.</u> New York: St. Martin's Press.

"Asserting Life Across New England, People Reach Out for Normalcy." <u>The Boston Globe.</u> 19 Sep 2001, Sec.B:1.

Bush, George W. (2001). <u>Our Mission and Our Moment.</u> New York: Newmarket Press.

"Educators, Historians Try to Make Sense of Sept 11." <u>Telegraph Herald (Dubuque, IA).</u> 10 March 2002, Sec.B:13.

"Emergency Director: Be Prepared for Terrorism." <u>Tampa Tribune.</u> 18 Oct 2001, Sec.PASCO:2.

"Emmy Awards are Postponed 'Out of Respect'." <u>The Houston Chronicle.</u> 12 Sep 2001, Sec.HOUSTON:1.

"Fear and Loathing; America was Supposed to be Their Safe Haven." The San Diego Union-Tribune. 29 Sep 2001, Sec.E:1.

"Old Glory, New Garb; Teens Wear Their Feelings in Red, White, Blue" The Washington Post. 23 Sep 2001, Sec.C:5.

Osofsky, Joy D. (1997). Children in a Violent Society. New York: Guilford Press.

Peale, Norman V. (1990). My Favorite Quotations. San Francisco: Harper & Row.

"Psychiatric Aftermath of Sept. 11 Will Take Time to Heal, Professionals Say." St. Louis Post-Dispatch. 26 Sep 2001, Sec.St. Charles County Post:2.

"Radio Address by the President to the Nation." The   Whitehouse. www.whitehouse.gov/news/releases/2002/03/2002031 6.html (04 Apr 2002).

"Rhetoric Toned Down as Football Returns." The Hartford Courant. 23 Sep 2001, Sec.E:7.

"Tennessee to Teach Sept. 11 in History by Fall." The Tennessean. 11 Feb 2002, Sec.B:1.

"Terror Cells Immersed in U.S. Life." The Baltimore Sun. 23 Sep 2001, Sec.A:13.

"Terrorist Attacks; The Impact; Kids Can Cope Differently, Depending on Their Ages." Newsday (New York). 12 Sep 2001, Sec.W:39.

"The Face of the Front: These Are Not Your Father's Armed Forces." Seattle Times. 20 Nov 2001, Sec.DOMESTIC NEWS.

Erica Craigston

About the Author

The author, who writes under the pen name Erica Craigston, received her Bachelor's degree in University Studies from Middle Tennessee State University. Her academic and personal backgrounds are diverse. She is currently pursuing a Master's degree at Colorado State University and working on her third non-fiction book.

Printed in the United States
ᴺ6800001B

9 781403 361776